Lecture Notes in Computer Science 12082

More information about this series at http://www.springer.com/series/7407

Dhabaleswar K. Panda (Ed.)

Supercomputing Frontiers

6th Asian Conference, SCFA 2020
Singapore, February 24–27, 2020
Proceedings

Editor
Dhabaleswar K. Panda
Department of Computer Science
and Engineering
The Ohio State University
Columbus, OH, USA

ISSN 0302-9743   ISSN 1611-3349   (electronic)
Lecture Notes in Computer Science
ISBN 978-3-030-48841-3   ISBN 978-3-030-48842-0   (eBook)
https://doi.org/10.1007/978-3-030-48842-0

LNCS Sublibrary: SL1 – Theoretical Computer Science and General Issues

This Springer imprint is published by the registered company Springer Nature Switzerland AG
The registered company address is: Gewerbestrasse 11, 6330 Cham, Switzerland

Preface

As the share of supercomputers in Asia continues to increase, the relevance of supercomputing merits a supercomputing conference for Asia. Supercomputing Asia (SCA 2020) was planned to be an umbrella of notable supercomputing events that promote a vibrant HPC ecosystem in Asian countries. With over 600 speakers, participants, and exhibitors already pre-registered to attend, SCA20 was on course to be the biggest SCA conference yet. It was planned to be held during February 24–27, 2020, at Suntec Singapore Convention and Exhibition Centre. Unfortunately, the physical conference was canceled due to the COVID-19 pandemic. However, the current proceedings contain the list of papers selected under its technical paper program.

The technical program of SCA19 provided a platform for leaders from both academia and industry to interact and to discuss visionary ideas, important global trends, and substantial innovations in supercomputing. SCA19 was attended by over 700 delegates from over 20 different countries. In March 2017, the National Supercomputing Centre (NSCC) Singapore hosted the Supercomputing Frontiers (SCF 2017). NSCC expanded the scope of SCF by embarking on the first Supercomputing Frontiers Asia (SCFA) technical paper program at SCA 2018. NSCC was established in 2015 and manages Singapore's first national petascale facility with available HPC resources to support science and engineering computing needs for academic, research, and industry communities.

SCFA represents the technical program for SCA 2020, consisting of four tracks:

– Application, Algorithms, and Libraries
– Architecture, Network/Communications, and Management
– Data, Storage, and Visualization
– Programming Models and Systems Software

The submitted papers for the technical papers program went through a rigorous peer review process by an International Program Committee. A set of eight papers were finally selected for inclusion in these proceedings. The accepted papers cover a range of topics including file systems, memory hierarchy, HPC cloud platform, container image configuration workflow, large-scale applications, and scheduling. I would like thank all authors for their submissions to this conference. My sincere thanks to all Program Committee members for doing high-quality and in-depth reviewing of the submissions and selecting the papers for this year's program. I would like to thank the conference organizers for giving me an opportunity to serve this year's conference as the technical papers chair. To the readers, please enjoy these proceedings.

April 2020   Dhabaleswar K. (DK) Panda

Organization

Program Chair

Dhabaleswar K. (DK) Panda   The Ohio State University, USA

Program Committee

Ritu Arora	Texas Advanced Computing Center, USA
Costas Bekas	IBM Zurich, Switzerland
Hal Finkel	Argonne National Laboratory, USA
Piotr R. Luszczek	University of Tennessee at Knoxville, USA
Antonio Pena	Barcelona Supercomputing Center, Spain
Nathan Tallent	Pacific Northwest National Laboratory, USA
Pradeep Dubey	Intel Corporation, USA
Rajkumar Buyya	The University of Melbourne, Australia
Albert Zomaya	The University of Sydney, Australia
Kishore Kothapalli	IIIT Hyderabad, India
Jianfeng Zhan	Institute of Computing Technology (ICT), China
Amitava Majumdar	San Diego Supercomputing Centre, USA
Nikhil Jain	Google Inc., USA
Ron Brightwell	Sandia National Laboratories, USA
John Kim	Korea Advanced Institute of Science and Technology (KISTI), South Korea
Ryota Shioya	Nagoya University, Japan
R. Govindarajan	Indian Institute of Science Bangalore, India
Quincey Koziol	Lawrence Berkeley National Laboratory, USA
Amelie Chi Zhou	Shenzen University, China
Ugo Varetto	Pawsey Supercomputing Center, Australia
Fang-Pang Lin	National Center for High-performance Computing (NCHC), Taiwan
Olivier Aumage	Inria, France
Sunita Chandrasekaran	University of Delaware, USA
Bilel Hadri	King Abdullah University of Science and Technology, Saudi Arabia
Hai Jin	Huazong University of Science and Technology, China
Arthur Maccabe	Oak Ridge National Laboratory, USA
Naoya Maruyama	Lawrence Livermore National Laboratory, USA
Ronald Minnich	Google Inc., USA
Yogesh Simmhan	Indian Institute of Science Bangalore, India
Sandra Gesing	University of Notre Dame, USA

Contents

File Systems, Storage and Communication

A BeeGFS-Based Caching File System for Data-Intensive Parallel Computing

David Abramson$^{(\boxtimes)}$, Chao Jin , Justin Luong ,
and Jake Carroll

The University of Queensland, St Lucia, QLD 4072, Australia
{david.abramson, c.jin, justin.luong,
jake.carroll}@uq.edu.au

Abstract. Modern high-performance computing (HPC) systems are increasingly using large amounts of fast storage, such as solid-state drives (SSD), to accelerate disk access times. This approach has been exemplified in the design of "burst buffers", but more general caching systems have also been built. This paper proposes extending an existing parallel file system to provide such a file caching layer. The solution unifies data access for both the internal storage and external file systems using a uniform namespace. It improves storage performance by exploiting data locality across storage tiers, and increases data sharing between compute nodes and across applications. Leveraging data striping and meta-data partitioning, the system supports high speed parallel I/O for data intensive parallel computing. Data consistency across tiers is maintained automatically using a cache aware access algorithm. A prototype has been built using BeeGFS to demonstrate rapid access to an underlying IBM Spectrum Scale file system. Performance evaluation demonstrates a significant improvement in the efficiency over an external parallel file system.

Keywords: Caching file system · Large scale data analysis · Data movement

1 Introduction

In order to mitigate the growing performance gap between processors and disk-based storage, many modern HPC systems include an intermediate layer of fast storage, such as SSDs, into the traditional storage hierarchy. Normally, this fast storage layer is used to build a burst buffer that stages data access to the disk-based storage system at back-end [12, 16]. However, adding new tiers into the storage hierarchy also increases the complexity of moving data among the layers [17, 18].

The burst buffer can be provided on I/O or compute nodes of a cluster. The latter option, also called a node-local burst buffer [17, 18], equips each compute node with SSDs to decrease I/O contention to back-end storage servers. This leads to a deep hierarchical structure [12, 13] that contains, at the very least, a node private burst buffer and a shared external storage tier. To exploit hardware advances, many innovative software methods [5, 7, 16–18, 28–31] are proposed to utilize burst buffers efficiently. The management of node-local burst buffers has not been standardized. Some projects have investigated its use only for specific purposes, such as staging checkpoint data [7]

© Crown 2020
D. K. Panda (Ed.): SCFA 2020, LNCS 12082, pp. 3–22, 2020.
https://doi.org/10.1007/978-3-030-48842-0_1

and caching MPI collective I/O operations [5]. Other projects, including BurstFS [28] and BeeOND [3], create a temporary file system on the private storage of compute nodes. However, these solutions manage the burst buffer independently of back-end storage, and programmers need to handle the complexity of moving data between storage tiers explicitly.

These tiers of persistent storage are typically used for different purposes in an HPC environment. Normally, the privately-owned internal storage maintains transient data to achieve faster I/O rates. In contrast, persistent data for long-term usage is stored externally, often using a parallel file system. Managing both tiers separately increases programming difficulties, such as maintaining data consistency and worrying the efficiency of moving data between the tiers. In order to bridge these layers, several challenges need to be addressed. First, the internal storage is isolated to individual compute nodes. Aggregating these siloed storage devices is necessary to provide scalable bandwidth for staging data more efficiently. Second, striping data across compute nodes is essential to accelerate parallel I/O for HPC applications. Third, programmers should be freed from having to move data explicitly between the storage tiers. Fourth, exploiting data access patterns through the storage layers can improve the performance of accessing the external parallel file system.

In this paper, we discuss the integration of the internal and external storage using a uniform solution. In particular, the paper describes a caching file system that automates data movement between a node-local burst buffer and a back-end parallel file system. It is realized by extending an existing parallel file system, BeeGFS [2]. Data access is unified across the storage layers with a POSIX-based namespace. In addition, the caching system improves storage performance by aggregating bandwidth of private storage, and exploiting data locality across the tiers. Furthermore, it increases SSD utilization by sharing data between compute nodes and across applications. Leveraging the inherent strengths of BeeGFS, such as data striping and meta-data partitioning, the caching extension supports high speed parallel I/O to assist data intensive parallel computing. Data consistency across storage tiers is maintained using a cache-aware algorithm.

Specifically, this paper presents the following contributions:

- A BeeGFS-based caching file system that integrates node-local burst buffers seamlessly with the back-end parallel file system;
- A unified data access abstraction that automates data movement and improves I/O performance by exploiting data locality across storage tiers;
- The caching extension mechanism that leverages parallel file system strengths to support scalable bandwidth and high-speed parallel I/O on the burst buffer.

The rest of this paper is organized as follows. Section 2 discusses related work and our motivation. Section 3 introduces the design and architecture of BeeGFS caching system. Section 4 presents the implementation details. Section 5 illustrates the performance evaluation of the prototype. Our conclusions follow in Sect. 6.

2   Background and Related Work

Most HPC systems adopt a hierarchical storage system [17, 18] to make the tradeoff between performance, capacity and cost. Recently, fast storage, such as SSDs, have been added between memory and disks to bridge the performance gap. This leads to a deep hierarchical structure. The top tier, such as the burst buffer [12, 16], provides high performance data access, and is placed close to compute nodes for containing actively used data. The bottom tier maintains long-term data persistently using disk-based solutions to provide high storage capacity. With most existing solutions, the software systems that manage different layers work separately [17, 18]. Accessing a disk-based storage tier has been standardized using a parallel file system, such as Lustre [26] and GPFS [22]. The appropriate way of managing a burst buffer is still under research [17, 18, 28, 29]. Currently, the internal storage layer cannot be directly utilized by most back-end parallel file systems [17, 18]. There is a lack of automatic data movement between storage tiers, and this causes a significant overhead to users [17, 18].

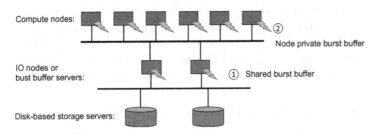

Fig. 1. Typical options of attaching a burst buffer.

2.1   Burst Buffer Overview

Currently, there are two major options to provide a burst buffer, as illustrated in Fig. 1. With the first option, compute nodes share a standalone layer of fast storage [16, 31, 33]. For example, the DoE Fast Forward Storage and IO Stack project [18] attaches the burst buffer to I/O nodes. Augmenting I/O nodes using SSDs improves bandwidth usage for disk-based external storage [31]. Cray DataWarp [10, 15] is a state-of-the-art system that manages a shared burst buffer, and it stages write traffic using a file-based storage space. Commands and APIs are supported for users to flush data from the burst buffer servers to the back-end file system. *Data elevator* [6] automates transferring data from the shared fast storage to the back-end servers. In addition, it offloads data movement from a limited number of burst buffer servers to compute nodes for scalable data transfer.

   Efficiently organizing data for burst buffers has been investigated [29–31]. Data is typically stored in a log-structured format, while meta-data is managed for efficient indexing using Adelson-Velskii and Landis (AVL) tree, hash table, or a key-value store. Optimizing the performance of flushing data to the external storage is critical. I/O interference can be prevented by leveraging the scalability of distributed SSD array.

Controlling concurrent flushing orders [30] and orchestrating data transfer according to access patterns [14] have been proposed. SSDUP [23] improves SSD usage by only directing random write traffic to burst buffers.

With the second option, the burst buffer is privately owned by each compute node [17, 18]. This approach provides scalable private storage and further decreases I/O contention to the back-end storage [20]. Presently, the software that manages a node-local burst buffer is not standardized. There are mainly two ways of utilizing node-local burst buffers. One approach exploits fast local storage only for specific purposes. For example, locally attached SSDs are used to cache collective write data by extending MPI-IO [5], and to build a write-back cache for staging checkpoint data [7]. Another approach provides a general file system service. Research has shown that deploying a parallel file system on compute nodes can substantially reduce data movement to the external storage [34]. Distributed file systems, such as HDFS [24], have explored using host-local burst buffers to support aggregated capacity and scalable performance. These solutions are designed mainly for scalable data access, and lack of efficient support for high performance parallel I/O required by most HPC applications. The ephemeral burst-buffer file system (BurstFS) [28] instantiates a temporary file system by aggregating host-local SSDs for a single job. Similarly, BeeGFS On Demand (BeeOND) [3] creates a temporary BeeGFS [1] parallel file system on the internal storage assigned to a single job. These file system solutions enable sharing a namespace across compute nodes at front-end, but it is separated from the back-end file system. Therefore, users have to transfer data between the internal and external storage layers explicitly.

2.2 Uniform Storage Systems for HPC Storage Hierarchy

A few projects share the same goals with our work. UniviStor [27] provides a unified view of various storage layers by exposing the distributed and hierarchical storage spaces as a single mount point. UniviStor manages the address space using a distributed meta-data service and hides the complexity of moving data across storage layers. In addition, adaptive data striping is supported for moving data in a load balanced manner. Hermes [13] supports a caching structure to buffer data in the deep memory and storage hierarchy transparently. With Hermes, data can be moved seamlessly between different layers, from RAM and SSDs to disks. Hermes places data across storage layers according to access patterns and supports both POSIX and HDF5 [9] interfaces. In comparison, our approach takes advantage of an existing parallel file system to achieve a similar outcome. By extending BeeGFS, we provide a caching system to integrate a node-local burst buffer seamlessly with an external storage.

2.3 Parallel File System Overview

POSIX-based parallel file systems, such as Lustre [26], GPFS [22], and PVFS [4], are widely used to manage a disk-based back-end storage system. Typically, parallel data access and scalable bandwidth are provided by aggregating storage servers. Normally, data is striped across servers and meta-data is partitioned to accelerate parallel I/O. BeeGFS [1] is a parallel cluster file system with the POSIX interface. BeeGFS manages meta-data and files separately and its architecture consists of meta servers, storage servers and management servers. BeeGFS transparently spreads data across multiple servers and scales up both system performance and storage capacity seamlessly. A single namespace is provided by aggregating all servers. File chunks are maintained by storage servers, whereas meta servers manage the meta-data, such as directories, access permission, file size and stripe pattern. Meta-data can be partitioned at the directory level such that each meta server holds a part of the file system tree. BeeGFS clients can communicate with both storage and meta servers via TCP/IP based connections or via RDMA-capable networks such as InfiniBand (IB). In addition, data availability is improved using built-in replication: buddy mirroring.

Managing a node-local burst buffer using a parallel file system can inherently leverage strengths, such as scalability and parallel data access, to assist data intensive computing. We extend BeeGFS to provide a caching system that bridges both internal and external storage tiers seamlessly. With the extension, BeeGFS allows moving data between the storage layers automatically. In addition, it improves data access performance by exploiting data locality across the storage tiers.

3 Design

The target environment consists of a compute cluster at the front-end and a persistent storage system at the back-end. Each compute node in the cluster is equipped with a large burst buffer, while the back-end storage system is managed using a POSIX-based parallel file system. Parallel applications running on compute nodes analyze data stored in an external file system. In order to decrease the I/O path of directly accessing the external system, hotspot data can be placed close to processors in the top tier of the storage hierarchy. Any applications running on the same cluster can access data stored in the burst buffer to reduce sharing data across programs using the external file system. Programmers are not required to know the exact location and long-term persistence for accessed files. In addition, to alleviate the performance gap between processors and storage, large files should be striped across compute nodes and serviced using parallel I/O. Moving data between the internal and external storage needs to be scalable with low I/O contention to avoid unnecessary network traffic.

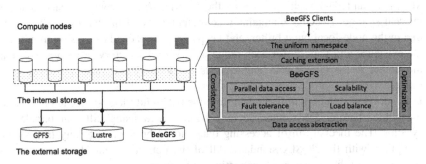

Fig. 2. The architecture of BeeGFS caching file system.

To meet these requirements, the fast storage isolated across compute nodes should be coordinated to provide a scalable caching pool. Each compute node contributes a part of its private storage and makes it accessible by other nodes. An instance of BeeGFS is deployed on the compute nodes to aggregate the siloed burst buffer. Managed by BeeGFS, the burst buffer stages data access for both write and read operations applied to back-end storage. Specifically, BeeGFS provides a parallel data service by accessing the targeted data set from an external file system. To improve performance, BeeGFS maintains most recently accessed files to avoid unnecessary network traffic and I/O to the back-end.

To provide a caching functionality, BeeGFS keeps track of accessed files. Whenever a file is requested, BeeGFS first verifies its existence and validity in the internal storage. In case a request cannot be satisfied due to a cache miss or an invalid copy, BeeGFS fetches data from the external file system transparently. Moving data, and examining its validity, are achieved using an on-demand strategy. If any updates need to be flushed to the external storage, BeeGFS synchronizes the permanent copy automatically.

Files are cached on compute nodes persistently, and are managed in a scalable manner by leveraging BeeGFS's scalability. In addition, BeeGFS organizes files with data striping and meta-data partitioning across the distributed fast storage to support high speed parallel I/O. When the free caching space is insufficient, least recently accessed files are evicted.

With the above design, programmers access files across storage tiers using a single namespace without worrying the exact data location, while data is committed for long-term usage automatically. Therefore, programmers are relieved from the complexity of manipulating data, but instead focusing on algorithm developments.

The architecture of BeeGFS caching system is illustrated in Fig. 2, which consists of two storage tiers. The top layer manages host-attached SSDs using BeeGFS. The bottom tier is the external storage cluster hosted by a parallel file system, such as GPFS, Lustre and others. To achieve the design targets, the following components extend BeeGFS to support the caching functionality:

- A POSIX-based uniform namespace: a uniform namespace across storage tiers enables accessing a piece of data regardless of its location. Most HPC applications rely on a traditional file interface. Therefore, providing a uniform namespace using the POSIX standard works with existing parallel applications seamlessly.
- Meta-data and data caching: files in the external file system are cached in the internal storage. BeeGFS maintains a consistent view of the back-end file system tree in the node-local burst buffer, and keeps track of cached objects by monitoring the existence and validity for each requested file and directory. It automatizes data movement across storage tiers, and exploits data locality to reduce unnecessary data traffic.
- Data access abstraction: moving data from the back-end file system can be achieved using file sharing. Each data site may be managed using different parallel file systems. The mechanism of accessing data should be applied to any file systems compliant with the POSIX standard. All of the data accessing details are hidden from users by the data access abstraction component.

- Data consistency: maintaining a coherent view between cached objects and their permanent copies needs to make an appropriate tradeoff between performance and consistency. Synchronizing updates should be optimized by avoiding unacceptable performance degradation.
- Optimization of data movement: moving data between the compute cluster and the external storage must be optimized with low I/O contention. Data transfer performance should be scalable with the number of involved compute nodes. In addition, data movement must take full advantage of high bandwidth and low latency of the storage network.

The performance target is to make both read and write operations applied to the external storage, with a cache hit, match the native BeeGFS on the burst buffer. With a cache miss, the read performance is restricted by the bandwidth of network and back-end storage. Accordingly, the extension should not change typical BeeGFS behaviors, such as high-performance data access, scalable storage capacity, load balancing and fault tolerance.

3.1 Uniform Namespace

The caching system provides a uniform namespace for accessing both internal and external files using the POSIX interface. Two sets of data are maintained in the internal storage: transient files and permanent files. The transient files require no long-term persistence, while each permanent file has a master copy in the external file system. Each file is referred using a local name, actually the full path. However, the local name for a permanent file also helps to identify its master copy in the external file system. This is achieved by linking an external directory to the internal file system, as illustrated in Fig. 3. In particular, each BeeGFS instance caches one external directory. The external director is specified when mounting the BeeGFS instance. The path name of the external directory is used to construct the external full path for each permanent file. Assume, a BeeGFS instance is mounted to the local directory */local/mounted* that caches files for an external directory */external/shared*. The local file */local/mounted/a. out* has an external copy */external/shared/a.out*, the name of which is produced by concatenating the external path, */external/shared*, and the relative path, *a.out*.

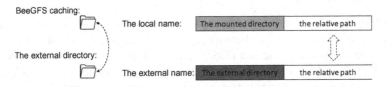

Fig. 3. Constructing the external path using the local name.

In another words, an internal directory is specified to hold the cache for an external data set. Actually, multiple external data sets, which may originate from different external file systems, can be linked to different internal directories. Therefore, the

POSIX file interface unifies storage access for both the internal burst buffer and external file systems. From the perspective of users, accessing the cached directory is no different than accessing other normal directories.

3.2 Caching Model

The caching model manages staging data for both read and write operations applied to the back-end parallel file system, and hides the details of moving data from users. In addition, it provides a consistent view on the shared external directory tree across storage tiers. For each cached object, its permanent copy maintained by the external file system is treated as the master version. To make an appropriate tradeoff between improving performance and enforcing data consistency, different strategies are applied to reading and writing files, and caching the namespace.

Writing files are staged using a write-back policy and reading files adopts a lazy synchronization method, in order to reduce unnecessary data movement. In contrast, the namespace is managed using an active strategy that guarantees a consistent global view across storage tiers. Reading the namespace is realized using an on-demand policy, while updating it is accomplished with a write-through method. The cache consistency is not controlled by the external file system, but actively maintained by the BeeGFS instance.

With the on-demand strategy, each level of the linked directory tree is cached only when it is traversed. When accessing a directory, all of its children directories are cached synchronously by duplicating its content to include name, creation time, update time, permission and size etc. However, files under the accessed directory are initially cached by only creating an empty position without copying the actual data. Subsequently, when the actual data is requested by any client, BeeGFS fetches the content to replace the empty position. Similar strategies are applied to synchronize updates made by the external file system.

To keep track of cached files and directories, BeeGFS meta-data, i.e. *inode*, is enhanced to include caching state and validity information. In addition, the creation and update times of the master copy are duplicated for consistency validation, the details of which is described in Sect. 3.3.

3.3 Data Consistency

The caching layer provides a two-level data consistency model to incorporate the performance difference between storage tiers. For concurrent data access applied to the internal storage layer, a strong and POSIX compliant consistency model is inherently supported by BeeGFS. Concurrent write operations can be coordinated by locking [2].

The caching model enforces data consistency between the cached objects and their permanent copies. Most scientific applications share data across clusters using a single writer model [1]. With this scenario, data is typically created by a single writer, even if it is shared with multiple writers across computer clusters. Accordingly, a weak consistency model is sufficient. The consistency is maintained per file. Validating the consistency is accomplished by comparing the update time between the cached object and its permanent copy. We assume each storage cluster uses a monotonically increasing clock to identify time for an update operation. In addition, the compute cluster and the back-end storage cluster may hold different clocks at the same time. The update time of an external file is denoted as *mtime*. When creating a cached copy, *mtime* is duplicated in its the meta-data, denoted as *mtime'*. During the lifetime of the cached object, *mtime'* does not change. At the back-end, *mtime* increases for each update applied to the permanent copy. Consequently, the validity of a cached object is examined using Eq. (1).

$$\begin{cases} \text{If } mtime' = mtime, \text{ the cached copy is valid.} \\ \text{If } mtime' < mtime, \text{ the cached copy is invalid.} \end{cases} \tag{1}$$

An invalid cached copy means that the master copy has been updated by the external file system. Therefore, synchronization is achieved by fetching the fresh copy from the external file system to replace the staled file in BeeGFS. This consistency semantic allows a single writer to spread its updates between multiple caching instances that share the same external directory tree.

3.4   Data Movement

Moving data across storage tiers should be parallelized to improve data transfer performance. Actually, data stored in the internal and external storage are both managed using parallel file systems. Files are striped across multiple servers and are serviced using parallel data access. Therefore, moving data across storage tiers should take advantage of both features. Instead of using any intermediate I/O delegates, each compute node should directly transfer file chunks that are managed by itself to the back-end storage. With this approach, the number of concurrent data transfer streams is scalable as the number of system nodes for both read and write operations. This type of highly parallel data movement can fully utilize the scalable bandwidth of storage network. In order to decrease I/O contention across files, transferring data can be ordered per file.

4   Implementation

The current prototype is implemented by augmenting the original meta-data and storage services. The meta server is extended to 1) keep track of each accessed object, 2) maintain data consistency between cached objects and their master copies in the external file system, and 3) coordinate staging data in and out of the internal storage. The storage server is improved to transfer data by leveraging BeeGFS data striping. The interaction of major caching components is illustrated in Fig. 4.

BeeGFS servers are implemented using C++, while its client is mainly written in C. BeeGFS clients, meta servers and storage servers communicate messages between each other using Unix sockets. Both meta and storage severs manage separate tasks using multiple worker threads. The caching extension expands the existing *inode* data structure and adds new messages and worker threads to achieve the design goal. The original BeeGFS structure is re-used as much as possible.

With the new BeeGFS caching system, both meta and storage servers are placed on compute nodes to manage the internal storage. Typically, one storage server is placed on each compute node, while the number of meta servers is configurable. The membership of BeeGFS cluster is maintained by a management service.

When mounting a BeeGFS instance, an external directory is linked, and it can be accessed using the Linux Virtual File System (VFS) interface. BeeGFS services VFS requests by accessing the external file system. For each VFS request, the BeeGFS client queries the meta-data service to determine if the target file exists internally. If an internal copy is valid, the request is serviced as normal. Otherwise, the meta server initiates moving the requested data to storage servers from the external file system.

4.1   Data Distribution

The caching extension re-uses the existing BeeGFS stripe formula to place all the chunks of a file across m storage servers in a round robin manner. Each cached file is uniformly partitioned into n chunks, and the size of each chunk is denoted *chunkSize*. The exact stripe formula is shown as Eq. (2):

$$offset(i) = i \times stripeSetSize + serverIndex \times chunkSize. \tag{2}$$

in which *stripeSetSize* $= m \times chunkSize$ and *offset*(i) stands for the ith stripe assigned to a storage server (identified by *serverIndex*).

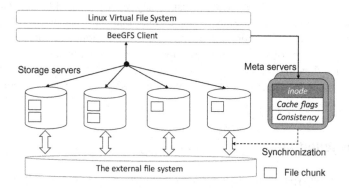

Fig. 4. The components of BeeGFS caching file system.

4.2   Meta Servers

The meta server coordinates storage servers to move data by adding new messages, such as *CachingFile*, and a worker thread *CacheEvictor*. The data structure that keeps track of cached objects must be persistent, otherwise, the caching system may become inconsistent in case of failures. Therefore, the existing BeeGFS data structures are re-used by leveraging its serialization logic to preserve included caching information persistently. The BeeGFS *inode* structure contains essential information, such as an *entry id*, which is used to identify each file and directory, the placement map for file chunks, and a feature field used for buddy mirroring. The *inode* structure is augmented to include the caching state for each file and directory, and to identify if the cached object is up-to-date. The feature field is extended to represent two flags: *caching* and *dirty*. The caching flag indicates if the associated file has a copy in the internal storage. *Caching* is *off* means that the file is created just for holding a position or has been evicted. After all the chunks of a file are duplicated in BeeGFS, *caching* is set *on*. The *dirty* flag is set when any update is applied to the cached copy. The master copy's *mtime* is also duplicated into *inode* for verifying the validity of a cached copy.

Namespace Consistency. Namespace coherence is maintained transparently using a polling approach to detect changes made by the external file system. However, an aggressive polling approach that periodically verifies the entire cached namespace causes a significant overhead for a deep directory tree. To implement an on-demand policy of enforcing consistency, a lazy polling approach is adopted that only examines the part of file system tree being traversed.

In particular, *stat*, *open*, *lookup* and *readdir* operations are intercepted. The external path name is reconstructed to validate the existence of the target item. If any new directory is detected, its content is cached immediately. For any new file created in the external directory, an internal entry is instantiated without copying the actual data. In addition, its *caching* flag is set *off* to indicate subsequent synchronization is required.

As described previously, updates applied to the internal directory tree are synchronized with the external file system using a write-through policy. Updates generated by operations, such as *chmod*, *chgrp*, *mv*, *rm* etc., are replicated to the back-end file system simultaneously. For a new file or directory created in BeeGFS caching, the external file system immediately holds a position for them. But the actual content is synchronized when required. BeeGFS exclusively partitions meta-data across multiple meta servers. Updates from different meta servers cause no conflicts.

Verifying namespace consistency changes the default behavior of read only meta-data operations, such as *stat*, *lookup* and *readdir*. These operations make no changes to the namespace in the original BeeGFS. However, with the caching extension, these operations may detect modifications on the external namespace, the synchronization of which causes updating the namespace cached in the internal storage.

File Consistency. File consistency is maintained by intercepting the *open* operation. Upon opening a file, the meta server queries its caching flag for the internal copy. In case the cached copy is present, its validity is examined using Eq. (1). If necessary, the master version is copied to replace the local stale one, which is coordinated by the meta server using a caching request. To avoid conflicts, multiple simultaneous *open* operations applied to the same file are serialized by the meta server. With this serialization, only a single caching request is created for one *open* operation and all other operations applied to the same file block until the requested file is ready to access. Synchronizing a file needs to update chunks that are distributed across storage servers. During the process, the target file should not be accessed, because its content may belong to different versions. Therefore, locking is used to protect file synchronization.

The transaction of moving or updating a file typically involves multiple storage servers. The exact process consists of two stages: 1) notifying all of involved storage servers and 2) moving file chunks. In the first stage, a *CachingFile* message is sent to all of the involved storage severs. The exact message includes file name, file size, and data stripe pattern etc. This stage is protected using a read lock. After sending the request, the second stage waits to start until all of the storage severs respond. At the end of the first stage, the read lock is released and a write lock is obtained immediately for the second stage. Both locks prevent other threads from opening the same file for updates until all the chunks have been successfully synchronized. After the secondary stage completes, the *open* operation continues as normal.

Optimization. Identifying an external file requires the concatenation of its internal path with the name of cached external directory, as illustrated in Fig. 3. However, reconstructing a path name in BeeGFS is not straightforward. BeeGFS does not keep a full path for any file or directory. In addition, meta-data for each entry is stored in a separate object, and each file is identified using its *entry id* and parent directory. Therefore, constructing the path name for a file or directory must look up each entry's parent backwards by going through a number of separated objects, which is time-consuming as it may require reloading the entry from storage. To improve the efficiency of verifying data consistency, constructing a path name is accelerated. When looking up a file from the root level, each parent entry is kept in memory for subsequent path construction.

4.3   Storage Servers

To assist file caching, eviction, and synchronization operations, BeeGFS storage servers are coordinated by the meta server. With file chunk distribution, each storage server only keeps a part of a cached file, and the storage server maintains each chunk using a local file. Upon receiving the request of transferring a file, the storage server creates the working directory on the internal storage and then initiates copying file chunks. Each storage server transfers data by only accessing a region of the target file from the external file system, instead of going through the whole file. In order to improve performance for accessing a file partially, instead of using *lseek, read* and *write* system calls, *pread* and *pwrite* are adopted. In addition, storage I/O access to the external file system must be efficient. The remote file is accessed using the recommended block size, which is detected using *stat*. Therefore, the exact data transfer is realized using a block-based algorithm, as shown in Algorithm 1.

Buddy Mirror. BeeGFS supports buddy mirroring to improve data reliability. Each group of buddy mirrors consists of two servers: the primary and secondary, in which each secondary server duplicates its primary counterpart. When the primary and secondary copies become inconsistent, it is required to synchronize buddies, which is called *resync*.

The caching module takes advantage of buddy mirroring to improve data availability, which is configurable, and to increase bandwidth for hotspot files. Presently, the replication for data caching is performed asynchronously such that the primary server does not wait until the secondary one finishes the caching request. However, the caching request must avoid interfering a resync process of buddy mirror. Specifically, caching requests are serviced until a resync process is completed.

Algorithm 1. The block-based data transform algorithm on the storage server.

1	**procedure** BLOCKIO (*fileDesc, buffer, len, offset, blocksize, isRead*)
2	$total = 0$
3	$bytes = 0$
4	**while** $total \leq len$ **do**
5	**if** $len - total < blocksize$ **then**
6	$iosize = count - total$
7	**else**
8	$iosize = blocksize$
9	**if** *isRead*
10	$bytes = pread$ (*fileDesc, buffer + total, iosize, offset + total*)
11	**else**
12	$bytes = pwrite$ (*fileDesc, buffer + total, iosize, offset + total*)
13	**if** $bytes \leq 0$ **then return** *error*
14	$total = total + bytes$
15	**return** *success*

4.4   Cache Eviction

When the free caching space is insufficient, some less accessed files should be evicted. Clean copies that are not updated in the caching, can be deleted directly. In contrast, for other dirty copies, updates should be flushed to the external file system.

The cache eviction routine is implemented by adding a worker thread, *CacheEvictor*, to the meta-data service, which is launched on startup with other worker threads. This eviction thread periodically selects less accessed files from storage servers that are low in space and moves them out of BeeGFS to keep available free space as required. The storage usage report created by the management service is re-used to detect the whole system storage usage. The management service monitors storage usage for each server and classifies them into *emergency, low* and *normal* capacity groups. The storage usage report is collected for each storage server periodically and sent to the meta servers. With this report, a Least Recently Used (LRU) policy is adopted to make decisions on which files should be moved out. Upon eviction, flushing dirty copies uses the same block-based data transfer algorithm as described in Sect. 4.3. A write lock is acquired to guarantee the eviction process is not interrupted by normal file operations.

5 Performance Evaluation

The prototype was built on BeeGFS version 6.1 and it was evaluated on the FlashLite system at the University of Queenland [8]. FlashLite contains large amounts of main memory and high-speed secondary storage, SSDs. The back-end storage is provided by an IBM Spectrum Scale (GPFS) system, and all compute nodes communicate with the GPFS system using the native Network Shared Disk (NSD) protocol [25]. High performance networking, such as Dual rail 56Gbps Mellanox InfiniBand fabric, connects FlashLite and GPFS servers. Each compute node of FlashLite has the following system configuration:

- 2 × Xeon E5-2680v3 2.5 GHz 12core Haswell processors;
- 512 GB DDR4-2133 ECC LRDIMM memory (256 GB per socket);
- 3 × 1.6 TB Intel P3600 2.5" NVMe (SSD) drives of internal storage;
- 1 TB RAID 1 system disk;
- 2 × Mellanox 56 Gb/s FDR Single Port InfiniBand adapter.

The CentOS 7 operating system, with kernel version 3.10.0–693, is installed on each node that manages SSDs using a standard *ext4* filesystem. The BeeGFS caching system was deployed for performance evaluation on 6 compute nodes of FlashLite. The system was installed with one meta server, one management server, and 6 storage servers. One BeeGFS storage server was placed on each compute node, while one compute node was selected to run both meta and management servers. The BeeGFS file system was mounted on each node at */mnt/beegfs* for caching a remote directory in GPFS. RDMA is enabled across the servers using the default BeeGFS OpenTk communication library. File chunk size was set to 512 KB, and a striping pattern RAID0 using four targets of storage server was specified. Buddy mirroring was disabled during the experiment. Performance was evaluated for both meta-data operations and file data accesses.

5.1 Meta-Data Performance

The performance of meta-data operations was evaluated using MDTtest [19]. MDTest measures meta-data performance through a series of *create*, *stat* and *delete* operations on a tree of directories and files. The operations were conducted in parallel on up to 6 compute nodes, in which each node run one MDTest instance. We compared these operations for three different situations: GPFS, BeeGFS caching prototype, and the original BeeGFS system (version 6.1). The vanilla BeeGFS system was installed on the same set of compute nodes in which the caching prototype was deployed, and was instantiated with the same configuration. MDTest was configured with a branch factor of 3, and a depth of 3. The number of items per tree node was set to 100, for a total of 4,000 files/directories per task. Each situation was evaluated using the number of performed transactions per second as metrics. The averaged value with a standard deviation was collected.

For read-only meta-data operations, such as *stat* for files and directories illustrated in Fig. 5, vanilla BeeGFS performs faster than GPFS, because it is deployed on internal storage. However, for write-intensive operations, such as creation and deletion of files and directories, as shown in Fig. 6 and Fig. 7 respectively, GPFS performs better than vanilla BeeGFS. This is because BeeGFS was created with only one meta-data server, which is not scalable for highly concurrent meta-data operations.

Overall, the caching prototype performs the worst for both read- and write-intensive meta-data operations. This is because the caching system not only conducts operations on internal storage, but also replicates these operations on the back-end storage. Our prototype performs both operations in a sequential manner, and this degrades performance. However, as shown in Sect. 5.2, the performance degradation has a negligible impact on the speed of accessing data in internal SSDs because meta-data operations only compose a tiny fraction of data access activities. Future work will investigate how to improve meta-data operations by maintaining consistency asynchronously.

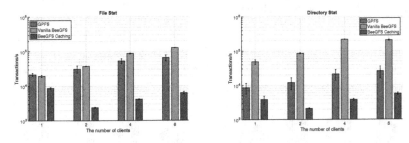

Fig. 5. MDTest file and directory stat.

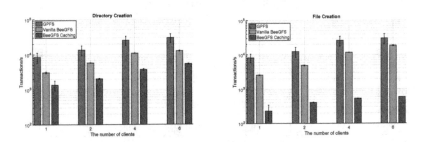

Fig. 6. MDTest file and directory creation.

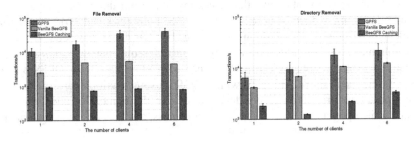

Fig. 7. MDTest file and directory removal.

5.2 Data Performance

Interleaved or Random (IOR) [10] was performed on the same set of compute nodes to evaluate the performance of accessing files stored in GPFS via the caching prototype. We compared two scenarios: cache miss and cache hit, for different file sizes, from 100 MB to 100 GB. One IOR client was placed on each compute node, while up to 6 IOR clients were used during the experiment. When a cache miss occurs, the requested file is fetched from back-end GPFS, while a cache hit means the requested file already stays in the BeeGFS caching system. In order to amortize the disturbance of other workloads present on GPFS, the IOR experiments were repeated over 24 h at hourly intervals. For testing read operations, the tested files were generated in advance and flushed out of the internal storage to enforce the behavior of cache-miss. The aggregated bandwidth perceived by multiple IOR clients was collected. The averaged values with a standard deviation were shown.

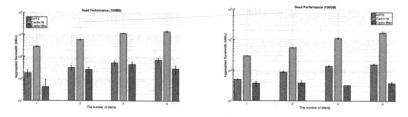

Fig. 8. IOR read performance.

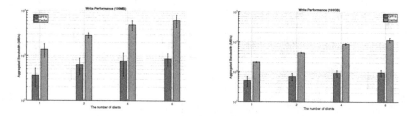

Fig. 9. IOR write performance.

Overall, the experiment shows that accessing data from the caching layer is significantly faster than directly accessing GPFS for both read and write operations, regardless of data size. In addition, accessing 100 GB large files delivers higher bandwidth than 100 MB files due to more efficient sequential operations on both internal and external storage. The performance of reading data from GPFS and the caching prototype is shown in Fig. 8, while Fig. 9 illustrates writing performance. The caching prototype provides scalable data access with the number of clients for both read and write operations. However, with a cache miss, the BeeGFS caching system is slower than GPFS because the requested data need to be copied into the internal storage first before being forwarded to applications. Therefore, the cache miss introduces an extra overhead in comparison to accessing GPFS directly. Future work will explore how to overlap data transfer across storage tiers to hide the extra latency for cache miss cases.

6 Conclusions

In order to improve storage performance, many HPC systems include an intermediate layer of fast storage, such as SSDs, between memory and the disk-based storage system. In particular, compute nodes may contain a large amount of fast storage for staging data access to the back-end storage. Frequently, this layer of node-local burst buffer is managed independently of the back-end parallel file system. To integrate the node-local burst buffer seamlessly with the existing storage hierarchy, we extend BeeGFS to provide a caching file system that bridges both internal and external storage transparently. Data access to the burst buffer and the back-end parallel file system is unified using a POSIX-based namespace. Moving data between the internal and external storage is automated and long-term data persistency is committed transparently. Accordingly, users are released from the complexity of manipulating the same piece of data across different storage tiers. In addition, the extension investigates how to utilize the burst buffer by leveraging the strengths of a parallel file system to accelerate data-intensive parallel computing. Taking advantage of BeeGFS, scalable I/O bandwidth is provided by aggregating siloed fast storage, and storage performance is improved by exploiting data locality across storage tiers. Data striping across storage servers not only supports high performance parallel IO, but also scales data transfer between storage tiers. In addition, a block-based algorithm increases the efficiency of data movement. The performance evaluation demonstrates that BeeGFS caching system improves data access significantly over directly accessing GPFS for both temporal and spatial locality patterns. However, the present prototype imposes additional overhead on meta-data operations due to maintaining data consistency between storage tiers synchronously. Our future work will explore how to reduce the extra overhead and apply the extension mechanism to other general parallel file systems.

Acknowledgements. We thank HUAWEI for funding this research project. We also acknowledge the University of Queensland who provided access to FlashLite. FlashLite was funded by the Australian Research Council Linkage Infrastructure Equipment Fund (LIEF).

References

1. Abramson, D., Carroll, J., Jin, C., Mallon, M.: A metropolitan area infrastructure for data intensive science. In: Proceedings of IEEE 13th International Conference on e-Science (e-Science), Auckland (2017)
2. BeeGFS. https://www.beegfs.io/content/. Accessed 21 Nov 2019
3. BeeOND. https://www.beegfs.io/wiki/BeeOND. Accessed 21 Nov 2019
4. Carns, P.H., Ligon III, W.B., Ross, R.B., Thakur, R.: PVFS: a parallel file system for Linux clusters. In: Proceedings of the 4th Annual Linux Showcase and Conference, pp. 317–327. USENIX, Atlanta (2000)
5. Congiu, G., Narasimhamurthy, S., Süß, T., Brinkmann, A.: Improving collective I/O performance using non-volatile memory devices. In: Proceedings of 2016 IEEE International Conference on Cluster Computing (CLUSTER 2016). IEEE, Taipei (2016)
6. Dong, B., Byna, S., Wu, K., Prabhat, J.H., Johnson, J.N., Keen, N.: Data elevator: low-contention data movement in hierarchical storage system. In: Proceedings of 23rd IEEE International Conference on High Performance Computing (HiPC). IEEE, Hyderabad (2016)
7. Dong, X., Xie, Y., Muralimanohar, N., Jouppi, N.P.: Hybrid checkpointing using emerging nonvolatile memories for future exascale systems. ACM Trans. Architect. Code Optim. (TACO) 8(2), 6:1–6:29 (2011)
8. FlashLite. https://rcc.uq.edu.au/flashlite. Accessed 21 Nov 2019
9. Folk, M., Heber, G., Koziol, Q., Pourmal, E., Robinson, D.: An overview of the HDF5 technology suite and its application. In: Proceedings of the EDBT/ICDT 2011 Workshop on Array Databases, pp. 36–47. ACM, Uppsala (2011)
10. IOR. http://wiki.lustre.org/IOR. Accessed 21 Nov 2019
11. Henseler, D., Landsteiner, B., Petesch, D., Wright, C., Wright, N.J.: Architecture and design of cray datawarp. In: Proceedings of 2016 Cray Users' Group Technical Conference (CUG 2016). Cray, London (2016)
12. He, J., Jagatheesan, A., Gupta, S., Bennett, J., Snavely, A.: DASH: a recipe for a flash-based data intensive supercomputer. In: Proceedings of the 23rd ACM/IEEE International Conference for High Performance Computing, Networking, Storage and Analysis (SC 2010), pp. 1–11. IEEE, New Orleans (2010)
13. Kougkas, A., Devarajan, H., Sun X.-H.: Hermes: a heterogeneous-aware multi-tiered distributed I/O buffering system. In: Proceedings of the 27th International Symposium on High-Performance Parallel and Distributed Computing (HPDC 2018), pp. 219–230. ACM, Tempe (2018)
14. Kougkas, A., Dorier, M., Latham, R., Ross, R., Sun, X.-H.: Leveraging burst buffer coordination to prevent I/O interferene. In: Proceedings of 12th IEEE International Conference on e-Science (e-Science 2017). IEEE, Baltimore (2017)
15. Landsteiner, B., Pau, D.: DataWarp transparent cache: implementation, challenges, and early experience. In: Proceedings of 2018 Cray Users' Group Technical Conference (CUG 2019). Cray, Stockholm (2018)
16. Liu, N., et al.: On the role of burst buffers in leadership-class storage systems. In: Proceedings of 28th IEEE Symposium on Mass Storage Systems and Technologies (MSST 2012). IEEE, San Diego (2012)
17. Lockwood, G.K., Hazen, D., Koziol, Q., et al.: Storage 2020: a vision for the future of HPC storage. Lawrence Berkeley National Laboratory (LBNL) Technical report, No. LBNL-2001072. NERSC (2017)

18. Lofstead, J., Jimenez, I., Maltzahn, C., Koziol, Q., Bent, J., Barton, E.: DAOS and friends: a proposal for an exascale storage system. In: Proceedings of the 29th ACM/IEEE International Conference for High Performance Computing, Networking, Storage and Analysis (SC 2016), pp. 807–818. IEEE, Salt Lake City (2016)
19. MDTest. http://wiki.lustre.org/MDTest. Accessed 21 Nov 2019
20. Nisar, A., Liao, W.-K., Choudhary, A.: Scaling parallel I/O performance through I/O delegate and caching system. In: Proceedings of the 21st ACM/IEEE International Conference for High Performance Computing, Networking, Storage and Analysis (SC 2008). IEEE, Austin (2008)
21. Ovsyannikov, A., Romanus, M., Straalen, B., Weber, G.H., Trebotich, D.: Scientific workflows at DataWarp-speed: accelerated data-intensive science using NERSC's burst buffer. In: Proceedings of 1st Joint International Workshop on Parallel Data Storage and data Intensive Scalable Computing Systems (PDSW-DISCS 2016), pp. 1–6. IEEE, Salt Lake City (2016)
22. Schmuck, F., Haskin, R.: GPFS: a shared-disk file system for large computing clusters. In: Proceedings of 1st USENIX Conference on File and Storage Technologies (FAST 2002). USENIX, Monterey (2002)
23. Shi, X., Li, M., Liu, W., Jin, H., Yu, C., Chen, Y.: SSDUP: a traffic-aware SSD burst buffer for HPC systems. In: Proceedings of the International Conference on Supercomputing (ICS 2017). ACM, Chicago (2017)
24. Shvachko, K., Kuang, H., Radia, S., Chansler, R.: The hadoop distributed file system. In: 26th IEEE Symposium on Mass Storage Systems and Technologies (MSST 2010). IEEE, Incline Village (2010)
25. Volobuev, Y.: GPFS NSD Server Design and Tuning, IBM GPFS Development Document, Version 1.0 (2015)
26. Wang, F., Oral, S., Shipman, G., Drokin, O., Wang, T., Huang, I.: 2010 Understanding Lustre Filesystem Internals, Oak Ridge National Laboratory Technical report, No. ORNL/TM-2009/117. National Center for Computational Sciences (2009)
27. Wang, T., Byna, S., Dong, B., Tang, H.: UniviStor: integrated hierarchical and distributed storage for HPC. In: Proceedings of 2018 IEEE International Conference on Cluster Computing (CLUSTER 2018). IEEE, Belfast (2018)
28. Wang, T., Mohror, K., Moody, A., Sato, K., Yu, W.: An ephemeral burst-buffer file system for scientific applications. In: Proceedings of the 29th ACM/IEEE International Conference for High Performance Computing, Networking, Storage and Analysis (SC 2016), pp. 807–818. IEEE, Salt Lake City (2016)
29. Wang, T., et al.: MetaKV: a key-value store for metadata management of distributed burst buffers. In: Proceedings of the 31st IEEE International Parallel and Distributed Processing Symposium (IPDPS 2017), pp. 807–818. IEEE, Orlando (2017)
30. Wang, T., Oral, S., Pritchard, M., Wang, B., Yu, W.: TRIO: burst buffer based I/O orchestration. In: Proceedings of 2015 IEEE International Conference on Cluster Computing (CLUSTER 2015). IEEE, Chicago (2015)
31. Wang, T., Oral, S., Wang, Y., Settlmeyer, B., Atchley, S., Yu, W.: BurstMem: a high-performance burst buffer system for scientific applications. In: Proceedings of the 2014 IEEE International Conference on Big Data (Big Data 2014). IEEE, Washington (2014)
32. Xie, B., et al.: Characterizing output bottlenecks in a supercomputer. In: Proceedings of the 25th ACM/IEEE International Conference for High Performance Computing, Networking, Storage and Analysis (SC 2012). IEEE, Salt Lake City (2012)

33. Zhang, W., et al.: Exploring memory hierarchy to improve scientific data read performance. In: Proceedings of 2015 IEEE International Conference on Cluster Computing (CLUSTER 2015), pp. 66–69. IEEE, Chicago (2015)
34. Zhao, D., et al.: FusionFS: toward supporting data-intensive scientific applications on extreme-scale high-performance computing systems. In: Proceedings of the 2014 IEEE International Conference on Big Data (Big Data 2014). IEEE, Washington (2014)

Multiple HPC Environments-Aware Container Image Configuration Workflow for Large-Scale All-to-All Protein–Protein Docking Calculations

Kento Aoyama[1,2], Hiroki Watanabe[1,2], Masahito Ohue[1],
and Yutaka Akiyama[1(✉)]

[1] Department of Computer Science, School of Computing,
Tokyo Institute of Technology, Tokyo, Japan
{aoyama,h_watanabe}@bi.c.titech.ac.jp,
{ohue,akiyama}@c.titech.ac.jp
[2] AIST-Tokyo Tech Real World Big-Data Computation Open Innovation Laboratory,
National Institute of Advanced Industrial Science and Technology,
Tsukuba, Ibaraki, Japan

Abstract. Containers offer considerable portability advantages across different computing environments. These advantages can be realized by isolating processes from the host system whilst ensuring minimum performance overhead. Thus, use of containers is becoming popular in computational science. However, there exist drawbacks associated with container image configuration when operating with different specifications under varying HPC environments. Users need to possess sound knowledge of systems, container runtimes, container image formats, as well as library compatibilities in different HPC environments. The proposed study introduces an HPC container workflow that provides customized container image configurations based on the HPC container maker (HPCCM) framework pertaining to different HPC systems. This can be realized by considering differences between the container runtime, container image, and library compatibility between the host and inside of containers. The authors employed the proposed workflow in a high performance protein–protein docking application—MEGADOCK—that performs massively parallel all-to-all docking calculations using GPU, OpenMP, and MPI hybrid parallelization. The same was subsequently deployed in target HPC environments comprising different GPU devices and system interconnects. Results of the evaluation experiment performed in this study confirm that the parallel performance of the container application configured using the proposed workflow exceeded a strong-scaling value of 0.95 for half the computing nodes in the ABCI system (512 nodes with 2,048 NVIDIA V100 GPUs) and one-third those in the TSUBAME 3.0 system (180 nodes with 720 NVIDIA P100 GPUs).

Keywords: Containers · Container image configuration · Singularity · Bioinformatics · Message passing interface

D. K. Panda (Ed.): SCFA 2020, LNCS 12082, pp. 23–39, 2020.
https://doi.org/10.1007/978-3-030-48842-0_2

1   Introduction

Containers that contribute to application portability through process isolation are now being widely used in computational applications. Today, many researchers run containers in various computing environments such as laptops, clouds, and supercomputers. Container technology is becoming essential for retaining scientific reproducibility and availability beyond system differences [1–3]. However, there remain certain limitations that need to be overcome to facilitate accurate configuration of container images for use in high-performance computing (HPC) applications running in multiple HPC environments. This requires users to understand systems, container runtimes, container image formats, and their compatibility with those used in HPC environments [4]. In addition, when an application establishes a message passing interface (MPI) communication over containers, the MPI library compatibility between the host system and the inside of the container must be ensured. This makes container deployment difficult. Therefore, these problems constitute a major obstacle facing the extensive use of the container technology in HPC environments.

To introduce the container's techniques and benefits to one of our HPC applications, MEGADOCK [5], the authors, in this study, propose use of a custom HPC container image configuration workflow. The said workflow is based on the HPCCM framework [6] to give users easier way to make containers when considering the specification differences between the hosts and containers in multiple HPC environments. Furthermore, we also showed the performance results of the containers configured using the proposed workflow in the target HPC environments with a large-scale dataset for over a million protein–protein pairs of docking calculations.

Key contributions of this research are listed hereunder.

– A container image configuration workflow for an all-to-all protein–protein docking application (MEGADOCK) for HPC environments is proposed.
– The workflow provides functions to customize container image configurations by considering specification differences between target HPC environments using the HPCCM framework.
– It has been confirmed that the parallel performance of containers configured using the proposed workflow exceeds a strong-scaling value of 0.95. The container was run with more than 2,000 GPUs for docking calculations of over a million protein–protein pairs.

2   Background

2.1   Containers for HPC Environment

Docker [7] is the most widely used container in general computing environments. Its usage ranges from personal development to large-scale production systems in cloud environments. This has been actively developed and great efforts have been made to standardize the container specification [8]. This, therefore, becomes a de-facto standard format of the containers.

However, in Docker's toolset design, there are several concerns about the performance overhead, operational policies, and affinity for traditional HPC software stacks, particularly those related to system privileges [9]. Owing to such concerns in the HPC community, other container environments have been proposed for use in HPC environments. These include Singularity [10], Shifter [11], Chariecloud [12], and Sarus [13]. They are operated on HPC systems, and benchmark performances of HPC containers indicate that they perform nearly at par with the bare-metal environment [14–16]. Those container environments provide similar features, for example, they do not require privileges for users, thereby solving the security concerns of HPC system policies unlike the general Docker environment[1]. In addition, they also support the 'pull' function which downloads a container image from general container registry services (e.g. Docker Hub [17]) and convert it to their own container image format.

Presently, the most emerging container environment in the HPC field is Singularity [10], which was originally developed by the Lawrence Berkeley National Lab and subsequently moved to Sylabs Inc. It provides runtime support for host GPU/MPI libraries to use those from the inside of the containers to meet the requirements of HPC applications. It also provides original container building toolsets along with its own registry service. This helps users upload container images for improving the preservability and portability of the application [18]. These functions make it easy for users to use host GPU devices with GPU-enabled container images that are available on Docker Hub, Singularity Hub [19], and NVIDIA GPU Cloud (NGC) [20].

Consequently, the number of HPC systems that provide container environments is constantly increasing. This is due to the widespread use of Singularity and other containers; however, there remain several difficulties in the deployment of containers in HPC environments. Some of these difficulties are described in the next section.

2.2   Problems of Container Image Configuration Workflow

Figure 1 describes an example of a typical container deployment workflow for several environments, including HPC systems.

HPC container deployment workflows are generally expected to support both Docker and Singularity to keep application portability in a wide range of computing environments. However, supporting both container environments from the level of container image specification (recipe) requires efforts for its maintenance. To this end, Singularity provides functions to download a container image from general registry services, and this image can be subsequently converted to Singularity's image format [10]. Therefore, it is possible to use various container images including Docker's images and run them on HPC systems using Singu-

---

[1] The `rootless-mode` is available from Docker 19.03 (since July 2019).

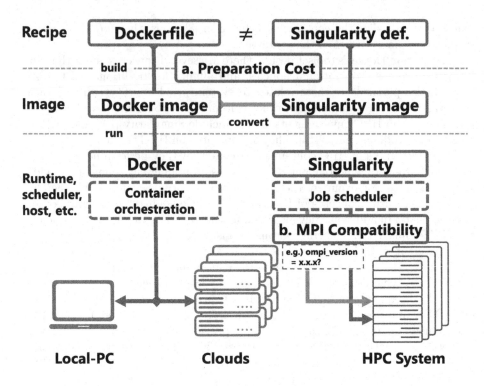

Fig. 1. Example of general container deployment workflow

larity. However, deployment of typical HPC applications nonetheless encounters several problems.

A. Preparation Cost for Container Image Recipe with Host Dependent Library. First, there exists a dependent library problem necessitating the availability of local libraries for using high-speed interconnects within target HPC systems. These must be installed within containers. For example, openib [25], ucx [26] or a similar library needs to be installed in the container if it is running on the system with InfiniBand [27]. On the other hand, the psm2 [28] library is required when it runs on the system with Intel Omni-Path [29].

Technically, it is possible to install almost all of the libraries in one container; however, it is generally not recommended as a best practice for container image configuration. Because most of the advantages of the containers originated from its light-weightiness, the containers must be as simple as possible.

B. MPI Library Compatibility for Inter-containers Communication. Second, if the process in a singularity container uses the MPI library to communicate with the process outside of the container, then the Application Binary Interface (ABI) must be compatible between MPI libraries of the host and container. For instance, it is necessary to install the same (major and minor) version of the library when OpenMPI [30] older than version 3.0 is used [2].

The problem pertaining to ABI compatibility can be overcome by using latest releases of MPI libraries, such as MPICH [31] v3.1 (or newer) or IntelMPI [32] v5.0 (or newer) given that they officially support compatibility between different library versions. However, users must know what version of MPI libraries are supported in both host systems and container images. Deployment of containerized MPI applications to HPC systems nonetheless involves large expenditures.

The above-mentioned problems are major difficulties to be considered when configuring the container image for the HPC environments.

3   HPC Container Maker (HPCCM) Framework

To solve these difficulties and ease the configuration of container specifications, use of the HPC Container Maker (HPCCM) framework was proposed by the NVIDIA corporation [6]. HPCCM is an open source tool to ease generation of container specification files for HPC environments. HPCCM supports both the Docker and Singularity specification formats via use of a highly functional Python recipe. This provides various useful functions to configure container images along with their application and system dependencies.

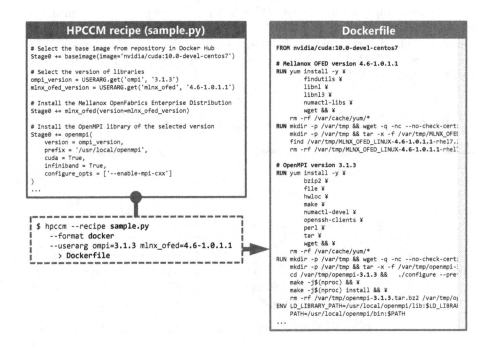

Fig. 2. Sample of HPCCM recipe and generated container specification (Dockerfile)

Figure 2 shows a sample Python recipe of HPCCM and a generated container specification in the 'Dockerfile' format. HPCCM contains the 'building blocks' feature, which transparently provides simple descriptions to install the specific components commonly used in the HPC community. Additionally, it supports flexible Python-based code generation functions, including recipe branch and validating user arguments; thus, it provides users with an easy method to generate the multiple container specifications from the same Python recipe file.

By adopting the HPCCM framework, the cost of container recipe preparation can be reduced by implementing one Python recipe and setting parameters of container specifications for HPC environments.

The authors used this HPCCM framework as a base for the proposed container deployment workflow for target HPC environments. The following section provides an overview of the target application and proposed workflow.

4   Container Deployment Workflow for MEGADOCK Application Using HPC Container Maker

4.1   MEGADOCK: A High Performance All-to-All Protein–Protein Docking Application

The authors selected MEGADOCK [5] as the proposed container configuration workflow application. MEGADOCK is an all-to-all protein–protein docking application written in C++/CUDA for use in large-scale computing environments. The internal process is based on Fast Fourier Transform (FFT) calculations for grid-based protein–protein docking using FFT libraries (e.g. FFTW [22], CUFFT [24]).

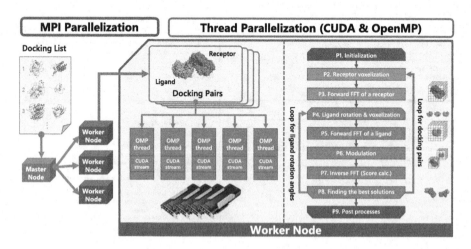

Fig. 3. Overview of docking calculations in MEGADOCK 5.0 (under development) and its OpenMP/GPU/MPI hybrid parallelization

In the latest implementation of MEGADOCK 5.0, which is under development, each docking pair calculation is independently assigned to an OpenMP [23] thread with CUDA streams [24]. The set of docking pairs is distributed by the master to workers in a typical master–worker framework implemented in C++ using the MPI library (Fig. 3).

At present, the authors are working toward improving the performance of the application as well as container portability in multiple environments while upgrading to the next MEGADOCK version. Currently, Docker images and their container specifications in the 'Dockerfile' format for GPU-enabled environments are provided to users having access to the MEGADOCK public repository on GitHub [33]. The authors reported scalable performance when operating those containers in a cloud environment using Microsoft Azure [34].

However, it is required to solve several container configuration difficulties when we assume the MEGADOCK application with Singularity containers on different HPC systems that are presented in previous sections. Therefore, the authors, in this study, propose use of an HPC container deployment workflow using the HPCCM framework. The said workflow supports a wide variety of computing environments and solves deployment problems in HPC systems for further advancement in this project.

4.2   HPC Container Workflow for MEGADOCK with HPCCM

Figure 4 provides an overview of the proposed container configuration workflow for deploying MEGADOCK in different HPC environments while using the HPCCM framework. Introducing the HPCCM framework in combination with the MEGADOCK application workflow offers the following advantages.

1. **Decreasing the cost of preparing container images**
   The workflow based on the HPCCM framework supports the configuration of container specifications in different environments by setting appropriate parameter values. Additionally, it supports both Docker and Singularity specification formats. This results in the reduction of management costs for container specification files, thereby facilitating continuous integration (CI) of container workflow.
2. **Avoiding library compatibility problems**
   The workflow provides a clear opportunity to specify the versions of dependent libraries by setting parameter values when container specifications are generated. Explicit and easy specifications of library versions help in overcoming problems associated with library compatibility. This is particularly true in cases where the exact version of the MPI libraries pertaining to the host HPC system and the inside of the container must match to avoid ABI compatibility issues.

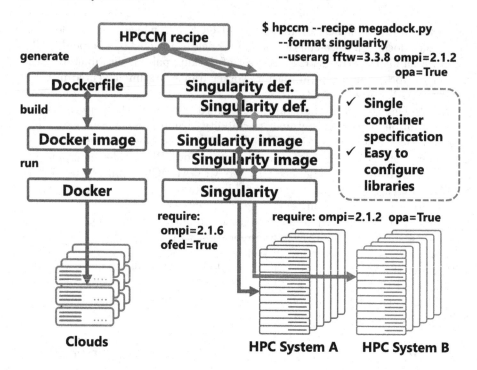

Fig. 4. Proposed HPC container deployment workflow for different HPC environments

4.3 Example of User Workflow

First, a user generates a custom container specification for both the target system and container environment by setting parameter values. Subsequently, the user builds a custom container image by using the container specification file in local environment (e.g. laptop, general cluster, etc.).[2]

Next, the user deploys custom containers to the target system for running the MEGADOCK application. Here, a user selects a compatible host MPI module and loads it while launching containers. The said containers can then communicate with processes over Singularity containers. Finally, custom containers pertaining to the MEGADOCK application distribute docking tasks via MPI communication in the target HPC system.

5   Evaluation Experiments

In this section, we evaluate the parallel performance of the custom containers in the target HPC environments. Container images were configured based

---

[2] This process can be skipped if there already exists a custom container image prepared for the target environment.

on the workflow proposed in the previous section. Additionally, we conducted a large-scale experiment involving over a million protein–protein pair docking calculations requiring a large number of computing nodes of the target HPC environment.

Target HPC environments used in both experiments correspond to ABCI (Table 1), located at the National Institute of Advanced Industrial Science and Technology, Japan, and TSUBAME 3.0 (Table 2), located at the Tokyo Institute of Technology, Japan. Both these environments provide Singularity environments and each computing node equips NVIDIA GPU devices; however, the systems have different hardware and software specifications.

Table 1. ABCI system hardware specifications

Item	Description	#
CPU	Intel Xeon Gold 6148, 2.4 [GHz]	×2
GPU	NVIDIA Tesla V100 for NVLink	×4
Memory	384 [GB]	
Local storage	NVMe SSD, 1.6 [TB]	×1
Interconnect	InfiniBand EDR, 100 [Gbps]	×2
Total number of computing nodes		×1,088

Table 2. TSUBAME 3.0 system hardware specifications

Item	Description	#
CPU	Intel Xeon E5–2680 v4, 2.4 [GHz]	×2
GPU	NVIDIA Tesla P100 for NVLink	×4
Memory	256 [GB]	
Local storage	NVMe SSD, 2.0 [TB]	×1
Interconnect	Intel Omni-Path HFI, 100 [Gbps]	×4
Total number of computing nodes		×540

5.1 Experiment 1. Container Deployment for Target HPC Environment

At first, we prepared custom container images for target environments and tested their execution performance using a small number of computing nodes with a benchmark dataset. The experiment aimed at validating the proposed workflow and ensuring that the custom container functions properly in the target environment.

System and Container Specifications. Specifications of the system software and container images used during experimentation are listed in Table 3.

Custom container images were prepared to those that are properly configured with the GPU/MPI libraries so they are compatible with the system modules [21] provided by the host (Table 3). The NVIDIA container image obtained from the Docker Hub (`nvidia/cuda:10.0-devel-centos7`) was selected as a base image because CUDA-10.0 [24] supports both GPU architectures in the target environments.[3]

Additionally, we installed each version of the OpenMPI [30] library by using different parameters to match the version of the host system module. The dependent libraries for the InfiniBand EDR [27] and the Intel Omni-Path HFI [29] were installed when necessary.

Table 3. Specifications of system software and container images used in Experiment 1

	ABCI	TSUBAME 3.0
System software specification		
OS	CentOS 7.5.1804	SUSE Linux Enterprise Server 12 SP2
Linux kernel	3.10.0	4.4.121
Singularity [10]	singularity/2.6.1	singularity/3.2.1
CUDA [24]	cuda/10.0/10.0.130	cuda/8.0.61
OpenMPI [30]	openmpi/2.1.6	openmpi/2.1.2-opa10.9
Container image specification		
Base image	nvidia/cuda:10.0-devel-centos7	nvidia/cuda:10.0-devel-centos7
FFTW [22]	fftw-3.3.8	fftw-3.3.8
CUDA [24]	cuda-10.0.130	cuda-10.0.130
OpenMPI [30]	openmpi-2.1.6	openmpi-2.1.2

Dataset. The dataset used during the experiment corresponds to the ZLab Docking Benchmark 5.0 [35]. We selected 230 files of the PDB (protein 3-D coordinates) format data labeled unbound. This was calculated for the protein–protein docking of the all-to-all ($230 \times 230 = 52,900$) pairs.

Computational Details. The input files are stored in a virtually distributed shared file system, called BeeGFS On Demand (BeeOND) [36], which is temporarily constructed on the set of non-volatile memory express (NVMe) storages in computing nodes. The output files are generated for each local NVMe storage

---

[3] The version of loaded CUDA modules were different in each environment; however, we confirmed that they did not exhibit any significant performance differences.

upon completion of each protein–protein pair docking calculation. When all calculations are completed, the output files are compressed as a `.tar` archive and moved to the global storage.

The measured execution time is obtained using the task distribution framework in MEGADOCK. This indicates the duration time from the start of task processing to the end of all tasks. The data point in the plot implies that each execution time is chosen from a median of three executions for the same calculations.

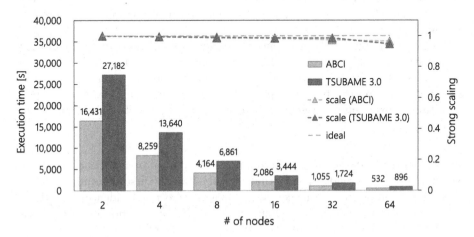

Fig. 5. Performance results of MEGADOCK docking calculations performed on ZLab Docking Benchmark 5.0 (all-to-all, 52,900 pairs) dataset in ABCI and TSUBAME 3.0 environments.

Results. Figure 5 depicts the performance results of the docking calculations using the benchmark dataset in both target environments. In all the docking calculations, no fatal errors were detected. The demonstration of the proposed custom container image configuration workflow was considered successful.

On average, the execution of the docking calculations in the ABCI environment was faster in comparison with that in TSUBAME 3.0 by 1.65 times at each point. The parallel performance in strong-scaling was found to be 0.964 on ABCI and 0.948 on TSUBAME 3.0 in the comparison of the execution time when running on 2 nodes versus 64 nodes. There are no significant differences between the environments in terms of scalability because the dataset used for this experiment was not sufficiently large.

The results obtained in the ABCI environment, which had four NVIDIA Tesla V100 devices, demonstrated better performance in comparison with TSUBAME 3.0 that comprised four NVIDIA Tesla P100 devices. This indicates that the performance of FFT-based docking calculations in MEGADOCK are computationally expensive, which heavily depends on the performance of the CUFFT library with the NVIDIA GPU, and therefore, the performance is directly affected by the host GPU device architecture.

5.2   Experiment 2. Performance Evaluation with Large-Scale Computing Nodes and over a Million Protein–Protein Pairs

Next, we performed a large-scale experiment using a larger number of computing nodes and over a million protein–protein pairs of docking calculations. To understand the principles of biological systems and elucidate the causes of diseases, over a million all-to-all protein pairs of docking calculations were considered in this experiment.

We reserved and used half of the computing nodes of the ABCI system (512 nodes with 2,048 GPUs) and one-third of the TSUBAME 3.0 system (180 nodes with 720 GPUs) for this experiment. The computational resources for calculations were supported by the "Grand Challenge" programs, which are open recruitment programs for researchers, coordinated by AIST and Tokyo Tech, respectively.

System and Container Specifications. Environmental specifications of the system hardware were identical to that described for the first experiment. Additionally, system software and container images were nearly identical to those corresponding to the first experiment. Several versions of libraries were modified, but no significant performance impact was observed.

Dataset. We used the dataset from the ZLab Benchmark 5.0 [35], which is the same as in the first experiment. To validate the large-scale application performance, we simply amplified the set of docking pairs to 25 times larger than the whole of the original dataset and created a virtual large-scale benchmark dataset. This dataset includes duplicated protein pairs; however, the docking calculations in the MEGADOCK application are completely independent of each other. Therefore, we computed 1,322,500 pairs of protein–protein docking calculations in total.

Computational Details. The application deployments, storage usage, and measurement methods are the same as in the first experiment.

As for the number of computing nodes used in each environment, we selected 16, 32, 64, 128, 256, and 512 nodes in the ABCI environment, and 90, 120, 150, and 180 nodes in TSUBAME 3.0. These node counts were set considering the limitation of reserved computational resources as well as performance predictions obtained from the previous experiment.

Results. Figure 6 depicts performance results obtained by performing large-scale docking calculations in the ABCI and TSUBAME 3.0 systems. The scale of computational resources and dataset size used in this experiment were larger

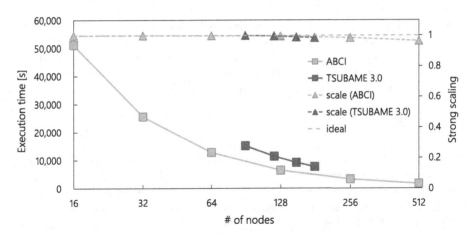

Fig. 6. Performance results of the MEGADOCK docking calculations with 1,322,500 pairs of proteins on ABCI and TSUBAME 3.0.

compared to the previous experiment; however, the parallel performance in both environments was observed to be similar.

The observed execution time equaled 1,657 s when using half the ABCI system (512 nodes with 2,048 NVIDIA V100 GPUs) and 7,682 s when using one-third of the TSUBAME 3.0 system (180 nodes with 720 NVIDIA P100 GPUs). A direct comparison of the performance in each environment is not warranted owing to differences between measured data points and computational resources. However, ABCI clearly demonstrated better overall performance.

The parallel performance in strong-scaling was found to be 0.964 on ABCI and 0.985 on TSUBAME 3.0 in the comparison of the execution time when running on each minimum-measured and maximum-measured number of computing nodes. This indicated that our container application workflow is able to achieve good scalability on the target HPC environments.

The older version of MEGADOCK required approximately half a day to run a million protein–protein pairs of docking calculations using the entire TSUBAME 2.5 system [5]. However, the latest MEGADOCK version completes over a million protein–protein docking-pair calculations within 30 min in the latest HPC environment.

6   Discussion

The proposed workflow considers ABCI and TSUBAME 3.0 as target HPC environments when deploying Singularity containers because they adopt similar architectural concepts but different specifications pertaining to both hardware and software. Thus, the environments are sufficient as targets for a proof-of-concept of our workflow.

Further, we can easily switch specific dependent libraries in each environment using the proposed workflow to fill gaps caused by differences in specifications. However, the proposed workflow does not cover other gaps, such as those pertaining to binary optimization of CPU/GPU architectural differences, MPI communication optimization for network architecture, and other performance optimization approaches. These features must be included in future implementations to enhance the utility of the proposed workflow.

7   Conclusion

In this study, the authors incorporated the HPCCM framework into a large-scale all-to-all protein–protein docking application called MEGADOCK to integrate the container deployment workflow over multiple HPC systems with different specifications. The proposed workflow provides users an easy means to configure containers for different systems and offers the flexibility to operate on both Docker and Singularity container formats. This helps users avoid container difficulties within HPC systems, such as host-dependent libraries and ABI compatibility of MPI libraries.

Further, we evaluated the parallel performance of container execution in both ABCI and TSUBAME 3.0 systems using a small benchmark dataset and a virtual large-scale datasets containing over a million protein–protein pairs. Result demonstrate that the parallel performance achieved exceeds a strong-scaling value of 0.95 when using half the ABCI system (512 nodes with 2,048 GPUs) and one-third of the TSUBAME 3.0 system (180 nodes with 720 GPUs). This demonstrates that the latest HPC environment can complete over a million protein–protein docking calculations within half an hour.

The authors believe that performance results obtained in this study can contribute to accelerate exhaustive large-scale 'interactome' analysis for understanding principles of biological systems. Additionally, the authors believe the proposed workflow would be beneficial for contributing to the portability of scientific achievements.

Code Availability. The entire source code of proposed container workflow and manual instructions are available in the following GitHub repository.

https://github.com/akiyamalab/megadock_hpccm

Acknowledgments. Computational resources of the AI Bridging Cloud Infrastructure (ABCI) were awarded by the ABCI Grand Challenge Program, National Institute of Advanced Industrial Science and Technology (AIST), and resource of the TSUBAME 3.0 was awarded by the TSUBAME Grand Challenge Program, Tokyo Institute of Technology.

This work was partially supported by KAKENHI (Grant No. 17H01814 and 18K18149) from the Japan Society for the Promotion of Science (JSPS), the Program for Building Regional Innovation Ecosystems "Program to Industrialize an Innovative Middle Molecule Drug Discovery Flow through Fusion of Computational Drug Design and Chemical Synthesis Technology" from the Japanese Ministry of Education, Culture, Sports, Science and Technology (MEXT), the Research Complex Program "Wellbeing Research Campus: Creating new values through technological and social innovation" from Japan Science and Technology Agency (JST), and conducted as research activities of AIST-Tokyo Tech Real World Big-Data Computation Open Innovation Laboratory (RWBC-OIL).

References

1. Zhang, J., Lu, X., Panda, D.K.: Is singularity-based container technology ready for running MPI applications on HPC clouds? In: Proceedings of the 10th International Conference on Utility and Cloud Computing (UCC 2017), Austin, TX, USA, pp. 151–160. ACM (2017). https://doi.org/10.1145/3147213.3147231

2. Veiga, V.S., et al.: Evaluation and benchmarking of Singularity MPI containers on EU research e-infrastructure. In: Proceedings of the 1st International Workshop on Containers and New Orchestration Paradigms for Isolated Environments in HPC (CANOPIE HPC), Denver, CO, USA, pp. 1–10. IEEE TCHPC (2019). https://doi.org/10.1109/CANOPIE-HPC49598.2019.00006

3. Paolo, D.T., Palumbo, E., Chatzou, M., Prieto, P., Heuer, M.L., Notredame, C.: The impact of Docker containers on the performance of genomic pipelines. PeerJ **3**(3), e1273 (2015). https://doi.org/10.7717/peerj.1273

4. Canon, R.S., Younge, A.J.: A case for portability and reproducibility of HPC containers. In: Proceedings of the 1st International Workshop on Containers and New Orchestration Paradigms for Isolated Environments in HPC (CANOPIE HPC), Denver, CO, USA, pp. 49–54. IEEE TCHPC (2019). https://doi.org/10.1109/CANOPIE-HPC49598.2019.00012

5. Ohue, M., Shimoda, T., Suzuki, S., Matsuzaki, Y., Ishida, T., Akiyama, Y.: MEGADOCK 4.0: an ultra-high-performance protein-protein docking software for heterogeneous supercomputers. Bioinformatics **30**(22), 3281–3283 (2014). https://doi.org/10.1093/bioinformatics/btu532

6. McMillan, S.: Making containers easier with HPC container maker. In: Proceedings of the SIGHPC Systems Professionals Workshop (HPCSYSPROS 2018), Dallas, TX, USA (2018). https://doi.org/10.5281/zenodo.3552972

7. Docker. https://www.docker.com/. Accessed 9 Dec 2019

8. Open Container Initiative. https://www.opencontainers.org/. Accessed 9 Dec 2019

9. Jacobsen, D.M., Canon, R.S.: Contain this, unleashing Docker for HPC. In: Proceedings of the Cray User Group (2015)

10. Kurtzer, G.M., Sochat, V., Bauer, M.W.: Singularity: scientific containers for mobility of compute. PLoS ONE **12**(5), 1–20 (2017). https://doi.org/10.1371/journal.pone.0177459

11. Gerhardt, L., et al.: Shifter: containers for HPC. J. Phys. Conf. Ser. **898**(082021) (2017). https://doi.org/10.1088/1742-6596/898/8/082021

12. Priedhorsky, R., Randles, T.: Charliecloud: unprivileged containers for user-defined software stacks in HPC. In: Proceedings of the International Conference for High Performance Computing, Networking, Storage and Analysis (SC 2017), Denver, CO, USA, no. 36, pp. 1–10. ACM (2017). https://doi.org/10.1145/3126908.3126925

13. Benedicic, L., Cruz, F.A., Madonna, A., Mariotti, K.: Sarus: highly scalable Docker containers for HPC systems. In: Weiland, M., Juckeland, G., Alam, S., Jagode, H. (eds.) ISC High Performance 2019. LNCS, vol. 11887, pp. 46–60. Springer, Cham (2019). https://doi.org/10.1007/978-3-030-34356-9_5

14. Torrez, A., Randles, T., Priedhorsky, R.: HPC container runtimes have minimal or no performance impact. In: Proceedings of the 1st International Workshop on Containers and New Orchestration Paradigms for Isolated Environments in HPC (CANOPIE HPC), Denver, CO, USA, pp. 37–42. IEEE TCHPC (2019). https://doi.org/10.1109/CANOPIE-HPC49598.2019.00010

15. Felter, W., Ferreira, A., Rajamony, R., Rubio, J.: An updated performance comparison of virtual machines and Linux containers. In: Proceedings of 2015 IEEE International Symposium on Performance Analysis of Systems and Software (ISPASS 2015), Philadelphia, PA, USA, pp. 171–172 (2015). https://doi.org/10.1109/ISPASS.2015.7095802

16. Xavier, M.G., Neves, M.V., Rossi, F.D., Ferreto, T.C., Lange, T., De Rose, C.A.F.: Performance evaluation of container-based virtualization for high performance computing environments. In: 2013 21st Euromicro International Conference on Parallel, Distributed, and Network-Based Processing, Belfast, pp. 233–240. IEEE (2013). https://doi.org/10.1109/PDP.2013.41

17. Docker Hub. https://hub.docker.com/. Accessed 9 Dec 2019

18. Sochat, V.: Singularity registry: open source registry for Singularity images. J. Open Source Softw. **2**(18), 426 (2017). https://doi.org/10.21105/joss.00426

19. Sochat, V., Prybol, C.J., Kurtzer, G.M.: Enhancing reproducibility in scientific computing: metrics and registry for singularity containers. PLoS ONE **12**(11), 1–24 (2017). https://doi.org/10.1371/journal.pone.0188511

20. NGC - GPU-Optimized Software Hub Simplifying DL, ML and HPC workflows. https://www.nvidia.com/en-us/gpu-cloud/. Accessed 9 Dec 2019

21. Furlani, J.L., Osel, P.W.: Abstract yourself with modules. In: Proceedings of the Tenth Large Installation Systems Administration Conference (LISA 1996), Chicago, IL, USA, pp. 193–204 (1996)

22. Matteo, F., Steven, G.J.: The design and implementation of FFTW3. Proc. IEEE **93**(2), 216–231 (2005). https://doi.org/10.1109/JPROC.2004.840301

23. Leonardo, D., Ramesh, M.: OpenMP: an industry standard API for shared-memory programming. Comput. Sci. Eng. **5**(1), 46–55 (1998)

24. Nickolls, J., Buck, I., Garland, M., Skadron, K.: Scalable parallel programming with CUDA. Queue GPU Comput. **6**(2), 40–53 (2008). https://doi.org/10.1145/1401132.1401152

25. OpenFabrics Alliance. https://www.openfabrics.org/. Accessed 11 Dec 2019

26. Unified Communication X. https://www.openucx.org/. Accessed 11 Dec 2019

27. InfiniBand Architecture Specification, Release 1.3.1. https://cw.infinibandta.org/document/dl/8125. Accessed 11 Dec 2019

28. intel/opa-psm2. https://github.com/intel/opa-psm2. Accessed 11 Dec 2019

29. Birrittella, M.S., et al.: Intel Omni-Path architecture: enabling scalable, high performance fabrics. In: 2015 IEEE 23rd Annual Symposium on High-Performance Interconnects, Santa Clara, CA, USA, pp. 1–9. IEEE (2015). https://doi.org/10.1109/HOTI.2015.22

30. Gabriel, E., et al.: Open MPI: goals, concept, and design of a next generation MPI implementation. In: Kranzlmüller, D., Kacsuk, P., Dongarra, J. (eds.) EuroPVM/MPI 2004. LNCS, vol. 3241, pp. 97–104. Springer, Heidelberg (2004). https://doi.org/10.1007/978-3-540-30218-6_19

31. MPICH. https://www.mpich.org/. Accessed 11 Dec 2019

32. Intel MPI Library. https://software.intel.com/mpi-library. Accessed 11 Dec 2019

33. akiyamalab/MEGADOCK. https://github.com/akiyamalab/MEGADOCK. Accessed 11 Dec 2019

34. Aoyama, K., Yamamoto, Y., Ohue, M., Akiyama, Y.: Performance evaluation of MEGADOCK protein-protein interaction prediction system implemented with distributed containers on a cloud computing environment. In: Proceedings of the 25th International Conference on Parallel and Distributed Processing Techniques and Application (PDPTA 2019), Las Vegas, NV, pp. 175–181 (2019)
35. Vreven, T., et al.: Updates to the integrated protein-protein interaction benchmarks: docking benchmark version 5 and affinity benchmark version 2. J. Mol. Biol. **427**(19), 3031–3041 (2015). https://doi.org/10.1016/j.jmb.2015.07.016
36. BeeGFS. https://www.beegfs.io/. Accessed 9 Dec 2019

DAOS: A Scale-Out High Performance Storage Stack for Storage Class Memory

Zhen Liang[1]([⊠]) [iD], Johann Lombardi[2] [iD], Mohamad Chaarawi[3] [iD], and Michael Hennecke[4] [iD]

[1] Intel China Ltd., GTC, No. 36 3rd Ring Road, Beijing, China
liang.zhen@intel.com
[2] Intel Corporation SAS, 2 rue de Paris, 92196 Meudon Cedex, France
johann.lombardi@intel.com
[3] Intel Corporation, 1300 S MoPac Expy, Austin, TX 78746, USA
mohamad.chaarawi@intel.com
[4] Lenovo Global Technology Germany GmbH, Am Zehnthof 77, 45307 Essen, Germany
mhennecke@lenovo.com

Abstract. The Distributed Asynchronous Object Storage (DAOS) is an open source scale-out storage system that is designed from the ground up to support Storage Class Memory (SCM) and NVMe storage in user space. Its advanced storage API enables the native support of structured, semi-structured and unstructured data models, overcoming the limitations of traditional POSIX based parallel filesystem. For HPC workloads, DAOS provides direct MPI-IO and HDF5 support as well as POSIX access for legacy applications. In this paper we present the architecture of the DAOS storage engine and its high-level application interfaces. We also describe initial performance results of DAOS for IO500 benchmarks.

Keywords: DAOS · SCM · Persistent memory · NVMe · Distributed storage system · Parallel filesystem · SWIM · RAFT

1   Introduction

The emergence of data-intensive applications in business, government and academia stretches the existing I/O models beyond limits. Modern I/O workloads feature an increasing proportion of metadata combined with misaligned and fragmented data. Conventional storage stacks deliver poor performance for these workloads by adding a lot of latency and introducing alignment constraints. The advent of affordable large-capacity persistent memory combined with a high-speed fabric offers a unique opportunity to redefine the storage paradigm and support modern I/O workloads efficiently.

This revolution requires a radical rethinking of the complete storage stack. To unleash the full potential of these new technologies, the new stack must embrace a byte-granular shared-nothing interface from the ground up. It also has to be able to

© The Author(s) 2020
D. K. Panda (Ed.): SCFA 2020, LNCS 12082, pp. 40–54, 2020.
https://doi.org/10.1007/978-3-030-48842-0_3

support massively distributed storage for which failure will be the norm, while preserving low latency and high bandwidth access over the fabric.

DAOS is a complete I/O architecture that aggregates SCM and NVMe storage distributed across the fabric into globally accessible object address spaces, providing consistency, availability and resiliency guarantees without compromising performance.

Section 2 of this paper describes the challenges that SCM and NVMe storage pose to traditional I/O stacks. Section 3 introduces the architecture of DAOS and explains how it integrates with new storage technologies. Section 4 gives an overview of the data model and I/O interfaces of DAOS, and Sect. 5 presents the first IO500 performance results of DAOS.

2 Constraints of Using Traditional Parallel Filesystems

Conventional parallel filesystems are built on top of block devices. They submit I/O through the OS kernel block I/O interface, which is optimized for disk drives. This includes using an I/O scheduler to optimize disk seeking, aggregating and coalescing writes to modify the characteristics of the workloads, then sending large streaming data to the disk drive to achieve the high bandwidth. However, with the emergence of new storage technologies like 3D-XPoint that can offer several orders of magnitude lower latency comparing with traditional storage, software layers built for spinning disk become pure overhead for those new storage technologies.

Moreover, most parallel filesystems can use RDMA capable network as a fast transport layer, in order to reduce data copying between layers. For example, transfer data from the page cache of a client to the buffer cache of a server, then persist it to block devices. However, because of lacking unified polling or progress mechanisms for both block I/O and network events in the traditional storage stack, I/O request handling heavily relies on interrupts and multi-threading for concurrent RPC processing. Therefore, context switches during I/O processing will significantly limit the advantage of the low latency network.

With all the thick stack layers of traditional parallel filesystem, including caches and distributed locking, user can still use 3D NAND, 3D-XPoint storage and high speed fabrics to gain some better performance, but will also lose most benefits of those technologies because of overheads imposed by the software stack.

3 DAOS, a Storage Stack Built for SCM and NVMe Storage

The **D**istributed **A**synchronous **O**bject **S**torage (DAOS) is an open source software-defined object store designed from the ground up for massively distributed Non Volatile Memory (NVM). It presents a key-value storage interface and provides features such as transactional non-blocking I/O, a versioned data model, and global snapshots.

This section introduces the architecture of DAOS, discusses a few core components of DAOS and explains why DAOS can be a storage system with both high performance and resilience.

3.1 DAOS System Architecture

DAOS is a storage system that takes advantage of next generation NVM technology like Storage Class Memory (SCM) and NVM express (NVMe). It bypasses all Linux kernel I/O, it runs end-to-end in user space and does not do any system call during I/O.

As shown in Fig. 1, DAOS is built over three building blocks. The first one is persistent memory and the Persistent Memory Development Toolkit (PMDK) [2]. DAOS uses it to store all internal metadata, application/middleware key index and latency sensitive small I/O. During starting of the system, DAOS uses system calls to initialize the access of persistent memory. For example, it maps the persistent memory file of DAX-enabled filesystem to virtual memory address space. When the system is up and running, DAOS can directly access persistent memory in user space by memory instructions like load and store, instead of going through a thick storage stack.

Persistent memory is fast but has low capacity and low cost effectiveness, so it is effectively impossible to create a large capacity storage tier with persistent memory only. DAOS leverages the second building block, NVMe SSDs and the Storage Performance Development Kit (SPDK) [7] software, to support large I/O as well as higher latency small I/O. SPDK provides a C library that may be linked into a storage server that can provide direct, zero-copy data transfer to and from NVMe SSDs. The DAOS service can submit multiple I/O requests via SPDK queue pairs in an asynchronous manner fully from user space, and later creates indexes for data stored in SSDs in persistent memory on completion of the SPDK I/O.

Libfabric [8] and an underlying high performance fabric such as Omni-Path Architecture or InfiniBand (or a standard TCP network), is the third build block for DAOS. Libfabric is a library that defines the user space API of OFI, and exports fabric communication services to application or storage services. The transport layer of DAOS is built on top of Mercury [9] with a libfabric/OFI plugin. It provides a callback based asynchronous API for message and data transfer, and a thread-less polling API for progressing network activities. A DAOS service thread can actively poll network events from Mercury/libfabric as notification of asynchronous network operations, instead of using interrupts that have a negative performance impact because of context switches.

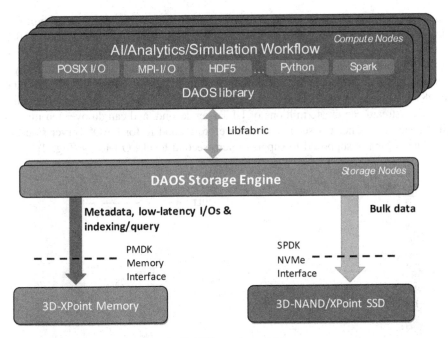

Fig. 1. DAOS system architecture

As a summary, DAOS is built on top of new storage and network technologies and operates fully in user space, bypassing all the Linux kernel code. Because it is architected specifically for SCM and NVMe, it cannot support disk based storage. Traditional storage system like Lustre [11], Spectrum Scale [12], or CephFS [10] can be used for disk-based storage, and it is possible to move data between DAOS and such external file systems.

3.2 DAOS I/O Service

From the perspective of stack layering, DAOS is a distributed storage system with a client-server model. The DAOS client is a library that is integrated with the application, and it runs in the same address space as the application. The data model exposed by the DAOS library is directly integrated with all the traditional data formats and middleware libraries that will be introduced in Sect. 4.

The DAOS I/O server is a multi-tenant daemon that runs either directly on a data storage node or in a container. It can directly access persistent memory and NVMe SSDs, as introduced in the previous section. It stores metadata and small I/O in persistent memory, and stores large I/O in NVMe SSDs. The DAOS server does not rely on spawning pthreads for concurrent handling of I/O. Instead it creates an Argobots [6] User Level Thread (ULT) for each incoming I/O request. An Argobots ULT is a lightweight execution unit associated with an execution stream (xstream), which is mapped to the pthread of the DAOS service. This means that conventional POSIX I/O function calls, pthread locks or synchronous message waiting calls from any ULT can block progress of all ULTs on an execution stream. However, because all building blocks used by DAOS provide a non-blocking user space interface, a DAOS I/O ULT will never be blocked on system calls. Instead it can actively yield the execution if an I/O or network request is still inflight. The I/O ULT will eventually be rescheduled by a system ULT that is responsible for polling a completion event from the network and SPDK. ULT creation and context switching are very lightweight. Benchmarks show that one xstream can create millions of ULTs per second, and can do over ten million ULT context switches per second. It is therefore a good fit for DAOS server side I/O handling, which is supposed to support micro-second level I/O latency (Fig. 2).

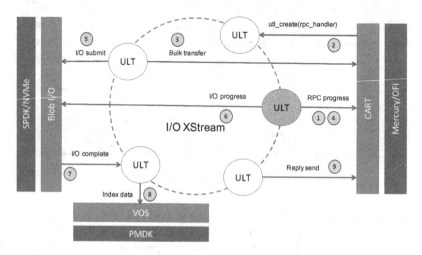

Fig. 2. DAOS server side I/O processing

3.3 Data Protection and Data Recovery

DAOS storage is exposed as objects that allow user access through a key-value or key-array API. In order to avoid scaling problems and the overhead of maintaining per-object metadata (like object layout that describes locality of object data), a DAOS object is only identified by a 128-bit ID that has a few encoded bits to describe data distribution and the protection strategy of the object (replication or erasure code, stripe count, etc.). DAOS can use these bits as hints, and the remaining bits of the object ID as a pseudorandom seed to generate the layout of the object based on the configuration of the DAOS storage pool. This is called algorithmic object placement. It is similar to the data placement technology of Ceph, except DAOS is not using CRUSH [10] as the algorithm.

This paper will only describe the data protection and recovery protocol from a high level view. Detailed placement algorithm and recovery protocol information can be found in the online DAOS design documents [5].

Data Protection

In order to get ultra-low latency I/O, a DAOS storage server stores application data and metadata in SCM connected to the memory bus, and on SSDs connected over PCIe. The DAOS server uses load/store instructions to access memory-mapped persistent memory, and the SPDK API to access NVMe SSDs from user space. If there is an uncorrectable error in persistent memory or an SSD media corruption, applications running over DAOS without additional protection would incur a data/metadata loss. In order to guarantee resilience and prevent data loss, DAOS provides both replication and erasure coding for data protection and recovery.

When data protection is enabled, DAOS objects can be replicated, or chunked into data and parity fragments, and then stored across multiple storage nodes. If there is a storage device failure or storage node failure, DAOS objects are still accessible in degraded mode, and data redundancy is recoverable from replicas or parity data [15].

Replication and Data Recovery

Replication ensures high availability of data because objects are accessible while any replica survives. Replication of DAOS is using a primary-slave protocol for write: The primary replica is responsible for forwarding requests to slave replicas, and progressing distributed transaction status.

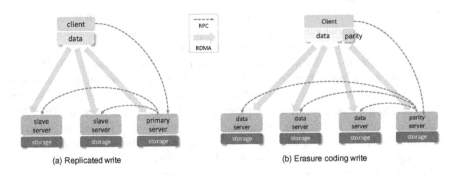

(a) Replicated write   (b) Erasure coding write

Fig. 3. Message and data flow of replication and erasure coding

The primary-slave model of DAOS is slightly different from a traditional replication model, as shown in Fig. 3a. The primary replica only forwards the RPC to slave replica servers. All replicas will then initiate an RDMA request and get the data directly from the client buffer. DAOS chooses this model because in most HPC environments, the fabric bandwidth between client and server is much higher than the bandwidth between servers (and the bandwidth between servers will be used for data recovery and rebalance). If DAOS is deployed for a non-HPC use case that has higher bandwidth between servers, then the data transfer path of DAOS can be changed to the traditional model.

DAOS uses a variant of two-phase commit protocol to guarantee atomicity of the replicated update: If one replica cannot apply the change, then all replicas should abandon the change as well. This protocol is quite straightforward if there is no failure.

However, if a server handling the replication write failed during the two-phase trans-action, DAOS will not follow the traditional two-phase commit protocol that would wait for the recovery of the failed node. Instead it excludes the failed node from the transaction, then algorithmically selects a different node as a replacement, and moves forward the transaction status. If the failed-out node comes back at some point, it ignores its local transaction status and relies on the data recovery protocol to catch up the transaction status.

When the health monitoring system of DAOS detected a failure event of a storage target, it reports the event to the highly replicated RAFT [14] based pool service, which can globally activate the rebuild service on all storage servers in the pool. The rebuild service of a DAOS server can promptly scan object IDs stored in local persistent memory, independently calculates the layout of each object, and then finds out all the impacted objects by checking if the failed target is within their layouts. The rebuild service also sends those impacted object IDs to algorithmically selected fallback storage servers. These fallback servers then reconstruct data for impacted objects by pulling data from the surviving replicas.

In this process, there is no central place to perform data/metadata scans or data reconstruction: The I/O workload of the rebuild service will be fully declustered and parallelized.

Erasure Coding and Data Recovery
DAOS can also support erasure coding (EC) for data protection, which is much more space and bandwidth efficient than replication but requires more computation.

Because the DAOS client is a lightweight library which is linked with the appli-cation on compute nodes that have way more compute resource than the DAOS ser-vers, the data encoding is handled by the client on write. The client computes the parity, creates RDMA descriptors for both data and parity fragments, and then sends an RPC request to the leader server of the parity group to coordinate the write. The RPC and data flow of EC is the same as replication: All the participants of an EC write should directly pull data from the client buffer, instead of pulling data from the leader server cache (Fig. 3b). DAOS EC also uses the same two-phase commit protocol as replication to guarantee the atomicity of writes to different servers.

If the write is not aligned with the EC stripe size, most storage systems have to go through a read/encode/write process to guarantee consistency of data and parity. This process is expensive and inefficient, because it will generate much more traffic than the actual I/O size. It also requires distributed locking to guarantee consistency between read and write. With its multi-version data model, DAOS can avoid this expensive process by replicating only the partial write data to the parity server. After a certain amount of time, if the application keeps writing and composes a full stripe eventually, the parity server can simply compute the parity based on all this replicated data. Otherwise, the parity server can coordinate other servers in the parity group to generate a merged view from the partial overwritten data and its old version, then computes parity for it and stores the merged data together with that new parity.

When a failure occurs, a degraded mode read of EC-protected data is more heavy-weight compared to replication: With replication, the DAOS client can simply switch to read from a different replica. But with EC, the client has to fetch the full data stripe and has to reconstruct the missing data fragment inflight. The processing of degraded mode write of EC-protected data is the same as for replication: The two-phase commit transaction can continue without being blocked by the failed-out server, instead it can immediately proceed as soon as a fallback server is selected for the transaction.

The rebuild protocol of EC is also similar to replication, but it will generate significantly more data movement compared to replication. This is a characteristic of all parity based data protection technologies.

End to End Data Integrity

There are three types of typical failures in DAOS storage system:

- Service crash. DAOS captures this by running the gossip-like protocol SWIM [13].
- NVMe SSD failure. DAOS can detect this type of failure by polling device status via SPDK.
- Data corruption caused by storage media failure. DAOS can detect this by storing and verifying checksums.

In order to support end-to-end checksums and detect silent data corruption, before writing the data to server the DAOS client computes checksums for the data being written. When receiving the write, the DAOS server can either verify the checksums, or store the checksums and data directly without verification. The server side verification can be enabled or disabled by the user, based on performance requirements.

When an application reads back the data, if the read is aligned with the original write then server can just return the data and checksum. If the read is not aligned with the original write, the DAOS server verifies the checksums for all involved data extents, then computes the checksum for the part of data being read, and returns both data and checksum to the client. The client then verifies the checksum again before returning data to the application. If the DAOS client detects a checksum error on read, it can enable degraded mode for this particular object, and either switch to another replica for the read, or reconstruct data inflight on the client if it is protected by EC. The client also reports the checksum error back to the server. A DAOS server will collect all checksum errors detected by local verification and scrubbing, as well as errors reported by clients. When the number of errors reaches a threshold, the server requests the pool service to exclude the bad device from the storage system, and triggers data recovery for it.

Checksums of DAOS are stored in persistent memory, and are protected by the ECC of the persistent memory modules. If there is an uncorrectable error in persistent memory, the storage service will be killed by SIGBUS. In this case the pool service will disable the entire storage node, and starts data recovery on the surviving nodes.

4 DAOS Data Model and I/O Interface

This section describes the data model of DAOS, the native API built for this data model, and explains how a POSIX namespace is implemented over this data model.

4.1 DAOS Data Model

The DAOS data model has two different object types: Array objects that allow an application to represent a multi-dimensional array; and key/value store objects that have native support of a regular KV I/O interface and a multi-level KV interface. Both KV and array objects have versioned data, which allows applications to make disruptive change and rollback to an old version of the dataset. A DAOS object always belongs to a domain that is called a DAOS container. Each container is a private object address space which can be modified by transactions independently of the other containers stored in the same DAOS pool [1] (Fig. 4).

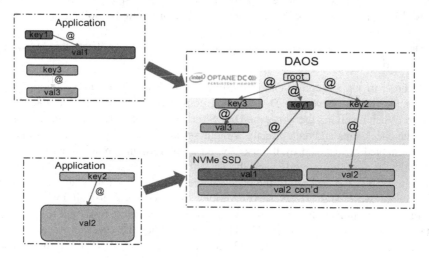

Fig. 4. DAOS data model

DAOS containers will be exposed to applications through several I/O middleware libraries, providing a smooth migration path with minimal (or sometimes no) application changes. Generally, all I/O middleware today runs on top of POSIX and involves serialization of the middleware data model to the POSIX scheme of directories and files (byte arrays). DAOS provides a richer API that provides better and more efficient building blocks for middleware libraries and applications. By treating POSIX as a middleware I/O library that is implemented over DAOS, all libraries that build on top of POSIX are supported. But at the same time, middleware I/O libraries can be ported to work natively over DAOS, bypassing the POSIX serialization step that has several disadvantages that will not be discussed in this document. I/O middleware libraries that have been implemented on top of the DAOS library include POSIX, MPI-I/O, and HDF5. More I/O middleware and frameworks will be ported in the future to directly use the native DAOS storage API.

4.2   DAOS POSIX Support

POSIX is not the foundation of the DAOS storage model. It is built as a library on top of the DAOS backend API, like any other I/O middleware. A POSIX namespace can be encapsulated in a DAOS container and can be mounted by an application into its filesystem tree.

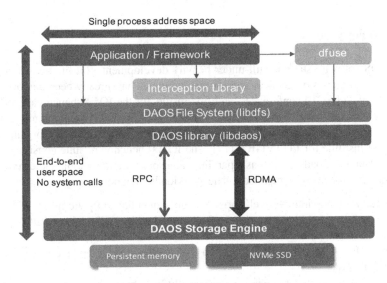

Fig. 5. DAOS POSIX support

Figure 5 shows the software stack of DAOS for POSIX. The POSIX API will be used through a fuse driver using the DAOS Storage Engine API (through `libdaos`) and the DAOS File System API (through `libdfs`). This will inherit the overhead of FUSE in general, including system calls etc. This overhead is acceptable for most file system operations, but I/O operations like read and write can actually incur a significant performance penalty if all of them have to go through system calls. In order to enable OS-bypass for those performance sensitive operations, an interception library has been added to the stack. This library will work in conjunction with dfuse, and allows to intercept POSIX `read(2)` and `write(2)` calls in order to issue these I/O operations directly from the application context through `libdaos` (without any application changes).

In Fig. 5, there is a layer between `dfuse`/interception library and `libdaos`, which is called `libdfs`. The `libdfs` layer provides a POSIX like API directly on top of the DAOS API. It provides file and directory abstractions over the native `libdaos` library. In `libdfs`, a POSIX namespace is encapsulated in a container. Both files and directories are mapped to objects within the container. The namespace container can be mounted into the Linux filesystem tree. Both data and metadata of the encapsulated POSIX file system will be fully distributed across all the available storage of the DAOS pool. The `dfuse` daemon is linked with `libdfs`, and all the calls from FUSE will go through `libdfs` and then `libdaos`, which can access the remote object store exposed by the DAOS servers.

In addition, as mentioned above, `libdfs` can be exposed to end users through several interfaces, including frameworks like SPARK, MPI-IO, and HDF5. Users can directly link applications with `libdfs` when there is a shim layer for it as plugin of I/O middleware. This approach is transparent and requires no change to the application.

5 Performance

The DAOS software stack is still under heavily development. But the performance it can achieve on new storage class memory technologies has already been demonstrated at the ISC19 and SC19 conferences, and first results for the IO500 benchmark suite on DAOS version 0.6 have been recently submitted [16]. IO500 is a community activity to track storage performance and storage technologies of supercomputers, organized by the Virtual Institute for I/O (VI4IO) [17]. The IO500 benchmark suite consists of data and metadata workloads as well as a parallel namespace scanning tool, and calculates a single ranking score for comparison. The workloads include:

- IOR-Easy: Bandwidth for well-formed large sequential I/O patterns
- IOR-Hard: Bandwidth for a strided I/O workload with small unaligned I/O transfers (47001 bytes)
- MDTest-Easy: Metadata operations on 0-byte files, using separate directories for each MPI task
- MDTest-Hard: Metadata operations on small (3901 byte) files in a shared directory
- Find: Finding relevant files through directory traversals

We have adapted the I/O driver used for IOR and MDTEST to work directly over the DFS API described in Sect. 4. The driver was pushed and accepted to the upstream ior-hpc repository for reference. Developing a new IO driver is relatively easy since, as mentioned before, the DFS API closely resembles the POSIX API. The following summarizes the steps for implementing a DFS backend for IOR and mdtest. The same scheme can also be applied to other applications using the POSIX API:

- Add an initialize callback to connect to the DAOS pool and open the DAOS container that will encapsulate the namespace. A DFS mount is then created over that container.
- Add callbacks for all the required operations, and substitute the POSIX API with the corresponding DFS API. All the POSIX operations used in IOR and mdtest have a corresponding DFS API, which makes the mapping easy. For example:
  - change `mkdir()` to `dfs_mkdir()`;
  - change `open64()` to `dfs_open()`;
  - change `write()` to `dfs_write()`;
  - etc.
  - Add a finalize callback to unmount the DFS mount and close the pool and container handle.

Two lists of IO500 results are published: The "Full List" or "Ranked List" contains performance results that are achieved on an arbitrary number of client nodes. The "10 Node Challenge" list contains results for exactly 10 client nodes, which provides a standardized basis for comparing those IO500 workloads which scale with the number of client nodes [3]. For both lists, there are no constraints regarding the size of the storage system. Optional data fields may provide information about the number and type of storage devices for data and metadata; when present in the submissions this information can be used to judge the relative efficiency of the storage systems.

For the submission to IO500 at SC19 [16], the IO500 benchmarks have been run on Intel's DAOS prototype cluster "Wolf". The eight dual-socket storage nodes of the "Wolf" cluster use Intel Xeon Platinum 8260 processors. Each storage node is equipped with 12 Intel Optane Data Center Persistent Memory Modules (DCPMMs) with a capacity of 512 GiB (3 TiB total per node, configured in app-direct/interleaved mode). The dual-socket client nodes of the "Wolf" cluster use Intel Xeon E5-2699 v4 processors. Both the DAOS storage nodes and the client nodes are equipped with two Intel Omni-Path 100 adapters per node.

Figure 6 shows the IO500 IOR bandwidth of the top four storage systems on the November 2019 edition of the IO500 "10-Node Challenge". DAOS achieved both the #1 overall rank, as well as the highest "bw" bandwidth score (the geometric mean of the four IOR workloads). Due to its multi-versioned data model, DAOS does not require read-modify-write operations for small or unaligned writes (which generates extra I/O traffic and locking contention in traditional POSIX filesystems). This property of the DAOS storage engine results in very similar DAOS bandwidth for the "hard" and "easy" IOR workloads, and provides predictable performance across many different workloads.

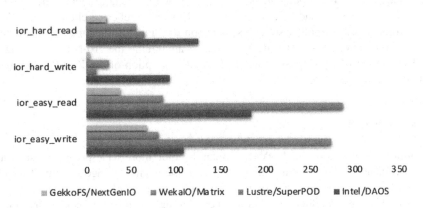

Fig. 6. IO500 10-node challenge – IOR bandwidth in GB/s

Figure 7 shows the mdtest metadata performance of the top four storage systems on the November 2019 edition of the IO500 "10-Node Challenge". DAOS dominates the overall "md" metadata score (geometric mean of all mdtest workloads), with almost a 3x difference to the nearest contender. This is mainly due to the lightweight end-to-end user space storage stack, combined with an ultra-low latency network and DCPMM storage media. Like the IOR bandwidth results, the DAOS metadata performance is very homogeneous across all the tests, whereas many of the other file systems exhibit large variations between the different metadata workloads.

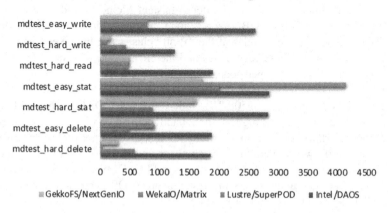

Fig. 7. IO500 10-node challenge – mdtest performance in kIOP/s

DAOS achieved the second rank on the November 2019 "Full List", using just 26 client nodes. Much better performance can be expected with a larger set of client nodes, especially for those metadata tests that scale with the number of client nodes. So a direct comparison with other storage systems on the "Full List" (some of which were tested with hundreds of client nodes) is not as meaningful as the "10-Node Challenge".

The full list of IO500 results and a detailed description of the IO500 benchmark suite can be found at Ref. [16].

6   Conclusion

As storage class memory and NVMe storage become more widespread, the software stack overhead factors more and more as part of the overall storage system. It is very difficult for traditional storage systems to take full advantage of these storage hardware devices. This paper presented DAOS as a newly designed software stack for these new storage technologies, described the technical characteristics of DAOS, and explained how it can achieve both high performance and high resilience.

In the performance section, IO500 benchmark results proved that DAOS can take advantage of the new storage devices and their user space interfaces. More important than the absolute ranking on the IO500 list is the fact that DAOS performance is very homogeneous across the IO500 workflows, whereas other file systems sometimes exhibit orders-of-magnitude performance differences between individual IO500 tests.

This paper only briefly introduced a few core technical components of DAOS and its current POSIX I/O middleware. Other supported I/O libraries like MPI-I/O and HDF5 are not covered by this paper and will be the subject of future studies. Additional I/O middleware plugins based on DAOS/libdfs are still in development. The roadmap, design documents and development status of DAOS can be found on github [5] and the Intel DAOS website [4].

References

1. Breitenfeld, M.S., et al.: DAOS for extreme-scale systems in scientific applications (2017). https://arxiv.org/pdf/1712.00423.pdf
2. Rudoff, A.: APIs for persistent memory programming (2018). https://storageconference.us/2018/Presentations/Rudoff.pdf
3. Monnier, N., Lofstead, J., Lawson, M., Curry, M.: Profiling platform storage using IO500 and mistral. In: 4th International Parallel Data Systems Workshop, PDSW 2019 (2019). https://conferences.computer.org/sc19w/2019/pdfs/PDSW2019-6YFSp9XMTx6Zb1FALM AAsH/5PVXONjoBjWD2nQgL1MuB3/6lk0OhJlEPG2bUdbXXPPoq.pdf
4. DAOS. https://wiki.hpdd.intel.com/display/DC/DAOS+Community+Home
5. DAOS github. https://github.com/daos-stack/daos
6. Seo, S., et al.: Argobots: a lightweight low-level threading and tasking framework. IEEE Trans. Parallel Distrib. Syst. 29(3) (2018). https://doi.org/10.1109/tpds.2017.2766062
7. SPDK. https://spdk.io/
8. Libfabric. https://ofiwg.github.io/libfabric/
9. Mercury. https://mercury-hpc.github.io/documentation/
10. Weil, S.A., Brandt, S.A., Miller, E.L., Maltzahn, C.: CRUSH: controlled, scalable, decentralized placement of replicated data. In: Proceedings of the 2006 ACM/IEEE Conference on Supercomputing, SC 2006 (2006). https://doi.org/10.1109/sc.2006.19
11. Braam, P.J.: The Lustre storage architecture (2005). https://arxiv.org/ftp/arxiv/papers/1903/1903.01955.pdf
12. Schmuck, F., Haskin, R.: GPFS: a shared-disk file system for large computing clusters. In: Proceedings of the First USENIX Conference on File and Storage Technologies, Monterey, CA, 28–30 January 2002, pp 231–244 (2002). http://www.usenix.org/publications/library/proceedings/fast02/
13. Das, A., Gupta, I., Motivala, A.: SWIM: scalable weakly-consistent infection-style process group membership protocol. In: Proceedings of the 2002 International Conference on Dependable Systems and Networks, DSN 2002, pp. 303–312 (2002)
14. Ongaro, D., Ousterhout, J.: In search of an understandable consensus algorithm (2014). https://www.usenix.org/system/files/conference/atc14/atc14-paper-ongaro.pdf

15. Barton, E.: DAOS: an architecture for extreme storage scale storage (2015). https://www.snia.org/sites/default/files/SDC15_presentations/dist_sys/EricBarton_DAOS_Architecture_Extreme_Scale.pdf
16. IO500 List, November 2019. https://www.vi4io.org/io500/list/19-11/start
17. Kunkel, J., et al.: Virtual institute for I/O. https://www.vi4io.org/start

Cloud Platform Optimization for HPC

Aman Verma[✉]

Microsoft, Redmond, WA 98052, USA
Verma.Aman@microsoft.com

Abstract. The special requirements of HPC have typically been tacked onto existing cloud infrastructure and practices. As a result, most cloud offerings aren't completely optimized for HPC, or aren't yet feature-complete as far as traditional supercomputing experience is concerned. This work addresses the progress made in (1) optimizing the performance of HPC workloads in a cloud environment, and (2) evolving the usability of cloud HPC environments. Specifically, this work discusses efforts made to minimize and eliminate the impact of virtualization on HPC workloads on cloud infrastructure and move towards a more familiar supercomputing experience. Initial experience with "cloud-native" HPC is also discussed. In many aspects, this work is inspired by and impactful for many HPC workloads in many disciplines including earth sciences and manufacturing.

Keywords: HPC · Cloud · Performance · Scalability

1 Introduction

The advent of cloud computing offers the promise of virtually unlimited resources, elasticity in scale, available on demand, with the appeal of access to the latest advances in technology in both hardware and software. The availability, flexibility and elasticity of cloud computing makes it appealing to a wide variety of workloads, including those in science and engineering. Many of the problems in the domain of scientific computing generally fall in at least one of the following 2 classes: (1) simulation of modeled representation of the physical world (computational physics, chemistry, mechanics, etc.), and (2) analysis of large amount of data (astrophysics, genomics, etc.). Both classes of problems, but more so the first have special demands on the computing infrastructure compared to other non-scientific computing workloads. Hence, many of these computing-intensive scientific computing workloads resort to "high performance computing (HPC)" primarily to minimize the time to solution or "time-to-science".

Cloud infrastructure has had to adapt to meet the "high performance" requirements of such workloads but mostly as an afterthought. This is primarily due to the fact that the vast majority of the public cloud as we know it had been built for, and has evolved out of the demand for consumer applications such as hosting websites, databases, object storage, content delivery, gaming, etc. Virtualization is one of the key technologies that has enabled the simulation and pooling of multiple dedicated resources from limited physical hardware. Hence virtualization is a common technology adopted

D. K. Panda (Ed.): SCFA 2020, LNCS 12082, pp. 55–64, 2020.
https://doi.org/10.1007/978-3-030-48842-0_4

by cloud providers to reduce hardware, save energy and offer more customized resource options to customers at attractive price points while leveraging the economies of scale.

Given all its advantages though, virtualization does not come free and incurs resource overhead. Ultimately, this overhead must be accounted for within the same pool of physical hardware, leaving slightly reduced resources for the customer workload, or worse, noise or interruption adversely impacting the customer workload. This is in stark contrast to the bare-metal environments the HPC community has been used to, over decades, by dint of practice and familiarity. This work addresses the progress made in (1) optimizing the impact of virtualization on HPC workloads in a cloud environment, and (2) evolving the usability of cloud HPC environments. Specifically, this work discusses efforts made to minimize and eliminate the impact of virtualization on HPC workloads on cloud infrastructure and move towards a more familiar supercomputing experience. The impact of such work is felt resoundingly in all industries that (1) traditionally have always been at the forefront of advancing HPC capabilities, and (2) are currently undergoing an all-encompassing digital transformation leveraging cloud computing.

2   Existing Gaps

The special requirements of HPC have typically been tacked onto existing cloud infrastructure and practices. As a result, most cloud offerings aren't completely optimized for HPC, or aren't yet feature-complete as far as traditional supercomputing experience is concerned. The key gaps are in the areas of:

(1) minimizing and eliminating impact of the virtualization layer (hypervisor),
(2) bare-metal-like representation of the hardware to the workload, and
(3) the HPC software ecosystem.

While the third item concerns more with the readiness and usability of the environment, the first two items directly impact the performance of HPC workloads.

The first two "performance" related items can be addressed by truly bare-metal instances which many cloud providers offer, and which come with a different set of considerations. Another common theme among cloud providers is that they offer instances with specific features exposed natively, in as bare-metal a state as possible, through the virtualization layer. The implementations differ and so do the feature-set and underlying performance and ease of usage. The "usability" is commonly addressed through one of two ways: (1) ready-to-use operating system images, preloaded with the right drivers, packages and applications to use the features out of the box, and (2) scripts or instructions to enable and use features. Solution approaches to address the existing gaps as listed above are described in greater detail as follows.

3   Methods

The optimization performed on the cloud computing platform are described as follows.

3.1   Eliminate "Jitter"

One of the biggest concerns of running an HPC (or any) workload on shared resources such as on the cloud is that of reduced performance due to a "noisy neighbor". At least on the aspect of sharing compute resources, this can be rather trivially addressed by hosting only 1 customer virtual machine (VM) per compute node. While the economics of this depends on the specifications of the compute node and the customer workload, this arrangement makes complete sense for HPC workloads. Compute resource intensive workloads, such as in HPC and AI, should first scale up (on the same compute node) before scaling out (to multiple compute nodes). Hence providing a full compute node per customer VM eliminates the "noisy neighbor" issue.

The issue of minimizing and eliminating the impact of the hypervisor can be addressed separately for compute and networking. The compute resources allocated to the hypervisor can be separate from the compute resources allocated to the customer VM or workload. On Azure, where the hypervisor is essentially a very stripped down version of Windows Server, this is accomplished using Minroot [1] and CpuGroups [2]. Minroot is used to constrain and isolate the compute resources (host virtual processors) allocated to the hypervisor. CpuGroups is used to group, constrain and isolate the compute resources (host virtual processors) allocated to the customer VM(s). As Fig. 1 illustrates, in the case of HPC on Azure HB-series, there is 1 customer VM per node and the hypervisor resources (physical cores 0–3) are separate from the VM's resources (physical cores 4–63). The VM on this 64-core node sees 60 cores divided across 15 NUMA nodes, isolated from any interference or "jitter" from the hypervisor.

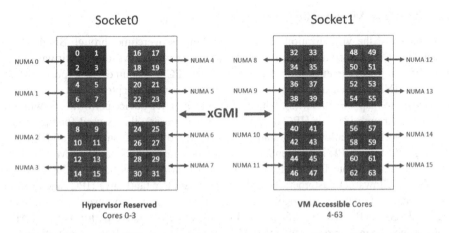

Fig. 1. Separation and isolation of the hypervisor from the VM to eliminate 'jitter'.

Performance jitter due to noisy neighbors in networking is a different topic but is an integral one when eliminating jitter holistically from a system. Such "networking jitter" can be trivially eliminated in a single node case when there is no inter-node communication over a network. However this trivial case is not interesting since the compute hypervisor jitter really manifests and becomes important when involving inter-node communication at a large enough scale. On Azure, the network jitter is attempted to be mitigated with the use of a balanced, non-blocking, fat-tree cluster and Adaptive Routing (AR) on the InfiniBand fabric [10]. With destination-based routing, AR enables the source node to select alternate paths to the same destination, allowing congested paths in the network to be avoided. This mitigation of networking jitter is demonstrated in Fig. 2 where enabling AR improves application (Star-CCM+) performance, particularly at scale on Azure HB-series with improvement up to 17% higher at 96 nodes when compared to AR disabled.

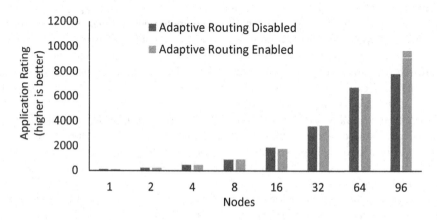

Fig. 2. Adaptive routing in the InfiniBand fabric mitigates "networking jitter".

3.2 Resource Virtualization

The impact of the virtualization on the networking is overcome through Single Root Input/Output Virtualization (SR-IOV). This technology allows device virtualization without using device emulation by enabling the PCIe resources to expose virtual functions (VFs) to virtual components (such as network adapter). This allows the hypervisor to map VFs to VM(s), which can achieve native device performance without using passthrough [3]. For HPC on Azure (e.g. HC-series), this is used for the InfiniBand network. This allows HPC and AI workloads to take advantage of all Message Passing Interface (MPI) implementations (and other frameworks based on MPI such as Horovod) and Remote Direct Memory Access (RDMA) verbs natively. SR-IOV for InfiniBand allows (1) customers to bring over a familiar (and any) HPC stack to the cloud, and (2) expose advanced networking features for optimized performance (HCOLL, SHARP, etc.). Figures 3 and 4 demonstrate the native performance of MPI point-to-point benchmarks – latency and bandwidth. This data is from running the OSU microbenchmarks with 3 MPI implementations: HPC-X, IntelMPI 2018, MVAPICH2 on Azure HC-series and HB-series for the latency and bandwidth tests respectively.

Complementary to the work above, performance with SR-IOV for InfiniBand had been shown to be comparable to that of bare-metal InfiniBand [4]. For compute

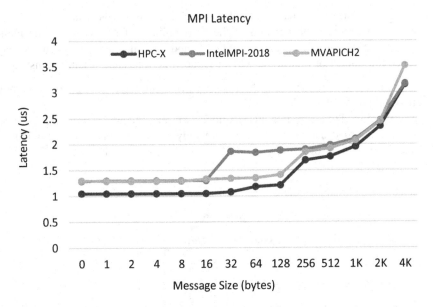

Fig. 3. Massive improvement in MPI latency due to platform updates, close to bare-metal performance expectations.

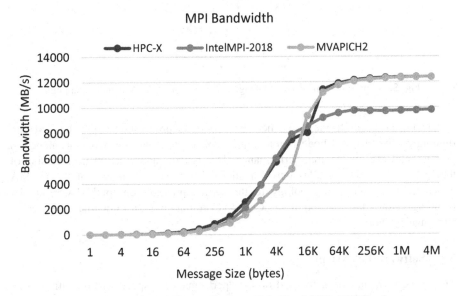

Fig. 4. MPI bandwidth near line rate (InfiniBand EDR 100 Gbps).

resources, there are other challenges with respect to mapping the physical CPU topology as-is to the virtual representation. This is especially important for chiplet-like designs with multiple NUMA nodes (or groups of L3-cache). On Azure HB-series and HC-series, the absence such mapping in a deterministic and inconsistent manner has resulted in differing performance of different realizations of the same experiment. Figure 5 is a fictional representation of the "scrambling" of the NUMA node numbering in the VM for a 2 socket, 16 NUMA node architecture. Applications may experience the impact of this in the way of reduced performance when, for instance:

- the data it was sharing with a NUMA node it was assuming to a neighbor is actually across an inter-socket link, or
- a process pinned to a core in a NUMA node assuming the NIC is affinitized nearby, attempts to broadcast message elsewhere only to realize that the bandwidth is reduced on account of the physical NIC being on a far NUMA node.

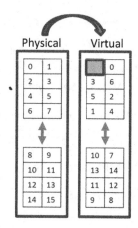

Fig. 5. Representation of the challenges of inconsistent NUMA node mapping.

Having an accurate view of where the workload processes (within the VM) are running on the physical node is important to plan out proper process placement and pinning, and eke out optimal performance. This issue is addressed in later version of the hypervisor which enables deterministic and consistent mapping of the NUMA nodes from the physical topology to the virtual presentation (pNUMA->vNUMA mapping). Note that corresponding pCore->vCore mapping at a granular core level is still ongoing work.

3.3   Software Ecosystem

The above work has been focused on the "performance" aspects of the platform; the "usability" side of the platform is equally important. Users of supercomputing facilities are accustomed to seeing pre-configured scientific computing and HPC packages available as ready-to-use, loadable modules. This greatly reduces the barrier to entry for new, first time users for such platforms, maintain control over the proliferation of custom environments, as well as provide some guarantees on function and performance of the various applications and packages. Spack is gaining popularity among system administrators of such facilities as a flexible package manager to support multiple versions, configurations, compilers and platforms.

An optimized, performant, and easy to use HPC software ecosystem allows customers to get native and designed-for performance right away. To this end, the following are made available on Azure:

(1) optimized VM OS images based on CentOS 7.6 and 7.7, with popular MPI implementations and scientific computing libraries [5],
(2) an optimized MPI implementation (MVAPICH2-Azure),
(3) native support for Open Container Initiative (OCI) format container images [6], including Singularity.sif image files
(4) recipes for scientific computing containers [7, 8], and
(5) Spack repo with integrated buildcache on Azure Blob (object storage) [11].

4   Results

The composite result of the progress made in (1) optimizing the performance of HPC workloads in a cloud environment, and (2) evolving the usability of cloud HPC environments is illustrated in Figs. 6, 7, 8 and 9. Figure 6 shows the performance of an open source reservoir simulator OPM Flow [9]. Expanding beyond the scope of traditional HPC applications, Fig. 7 shows the advantages offered by RDMA over InfiniBand for "big data" workflows leveraging SparkRDMA [12]. Figure 9 shows an example of running Horovod, a popular distributed AI training framework for TensorFlow; the efficiency of RDMA over InfiniBand outpacing that of IPoIB even at the relatively small scales. Both these experiments (Figs. 7 and 8) are performed on the Azure HC-series, with the Horovod experiment using Intel MPI. Finally Fig. 9 shows the scaling of a popular CFD application (Star-CCM+) up to 37000 cores on Azure HB_v2-series. This has now been extended to 57,000 cores which is a record run for HPC in the cloud.

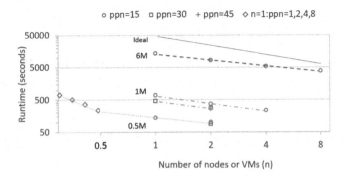

Fig. 6. Comparison of the runtime for the OPM reservoir simulator on HB with 3 different cases (0.5 M, 1 M and 6 M) for a combination of nodes and processes per node.

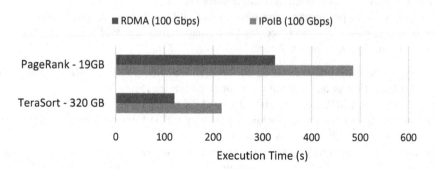

Fig. 7. Advantage of RDMA over InfiniBand for "big data" workloads using SparkRDMA.

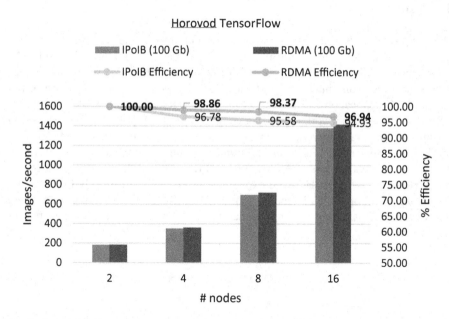

Fig. 8. Running Horovod, a distributed AI training framework for TensorFlow on an HPC platform.

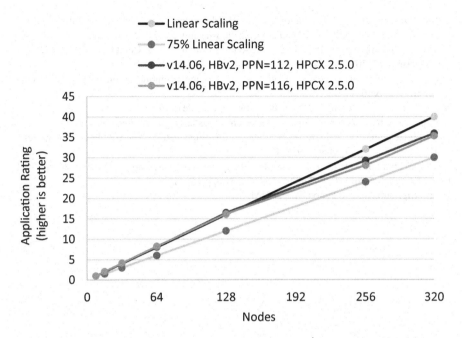

Fig. 9. Scaling of the CFD simulator Star-CCM+ up to 37000 cores.

5   Future Work

From an HPC platform perspective, the above work described the optimizations made for compute and clustered networking to enable not just the traditional HPC workloads, but also the emerging "big data" and AI workloads. A key piece of the puzzle to achieve complete parity with on-prem infrastructure, ecosystem and experience is HPC storage. While there is significant momentum in the convergence of HPC compute and networking to support the traditional HPC and AI workloads, the storage space appears to be evolving disjoint requirements and preferences. There may be a "divergence of HPC and AI" as far as storage is concerned, but this is evolving. There is ongoing work with "cloud-native" HPC which concerns "cloud-native" orchestration of resources, monitoring, logging, and interaction with distributed data stores.

References

1. https://docs.microsoft.com/en-us/windows-server/virtualization/hyper-v/manage/manage-hyper-v-minroot-2016
2. https://docs.microsoft.com/en-us/windows-server/virtualization/hyper-v/manage/manage-hyper-v-cpugroups
3. Efficient High-Performance Computing with Infiniband Hardware Virtualization. http://datas ys.cs.iit.edu/reports/2014_IIT_virtualization-fermicloud.pdf

4. SR-IOV Support for Virtualization on InfiniBand Clusters: Early Experience. http://mvapich. cse.ohio-state.edu:8080/static/media/publications/abstract/sriov-ccgrid13.pdf
5. https://techcommunity.microsoft.com/t5/Azure-Compute/Azure-CentOS-7-6-7-7-HPC-Images/ba-p/977094
6. https://techcommunity.microsoft.com/t5/Azure-Compute/Singularity-on-Azure-Containers-for-HPC/ba-p/464174
7. https://docs.nvidia.com/ngc/ngc-azure-setup-guide/index.html
8. https://github.com/vermagit/hpc-containers/tree/master/singularity/recipes
9. https://techcommunity.microsoft.com/t5/Azure-Compute/Reservoir-Simulation-on-Azure-HPC-for-Oil-amp-Gas/ba-p/791986
10. https://community.mellanox.com/s/article/How-To-Configure-Adaptive-Routing-and-SHIELD
11. https://github.com/Azure/azurehpc/tree/master/apps/spack
12. https://github.com/Mellanox/SparkRDMA

Applications and Scheduling

swGBDT: Efficient Gradient Boosted Decision Tree on Sunway Many-Core Processor

Bohong Yin[1], Yunchun Li[1,2], Ming Dun[2], Xin You[1], Hailong Yang[1(✉)],
Zhongzhi Luan[1], and Depei Qian[1]

[1] School of Computer Science and Engineering, Beihang University, Beijing, China
{15061139,lych,youxin2015,hailong.yang,07680,depeiq}@buaa.edu.cn
[2] School of Cyber Science and Techonology, Beihang University, Beijing, China
dunming0301@buaa.edu.cn

Abstract. Gradient Boosted Decision Trees (GBDT) is a practical machine learning method, which has been widely used in various application fields such as recommendation system. Optimizing the performance of GBDT on heterogeneous many-core processors exposes several challenges such as designing efficient parallelization scheme and mitigating the latency of irregular memory access. In this paper, we propose *swGBDT*, an efficient GBDT implementation on Sunway processor. In *swGBDT*, we divide the 64 CPEs in a core group into multiple roles such as *loader*, *saver* and *worker* in order to hide the latency of irregular global memory access. In addition, we partition the data into two granularities such as *block* and *tile* to better utilize the LDM on each CPE for data caching. Moreover, we utilize register communication for collaboration among CPEs. Our evaluation with representative datasets shows that *swGBDT* achieves 4.6× and 2× performance speedup on average compared to the serial implementation on MPE and parallel XGBoost on CPEs respectively.

Keywords: Gradient Boosted Decision Tree · Many-core processor · Performance optimization

1 Introduction

In recent years machine learning has gained great popularity as a powerful technique in the field of big data analysis. Especially, Gradient Boosted Decision Tree (GBDT) [6] is a widely used machine learning technique for analyzing massive data with various features and sophisticated dependencies [17]. GBDT has already been applied in different application areas, such as drug discovery [24], particle identification [18], image labeling [16] and automatic detection [8].

The GBDT is an ensemble machine learning model that requires training of multiple decision trees sequentially. Decision trees are binary trees with dual

© The Author(s) 2020
D. K. Panda (Ed.): SCFA 2020, LNCS 12082, pp. 67–86, 2020.
https://doi.org/10.1007/978-3-030-48842-0_5

judgments on internal nodes and target values on leaves. GBDT trains the decision trees through fitting the residual errors during each iteration for predicting the hidden relationships or values. Thus the GBDT spends most of its time in learning decision trees and finding the best split points, which is the key hotspot of GBDT [9]. In addition, GBDT also faces the challenge of irregular memory access for achieving optimal performance on emerging many-core processors such as Sunway [7].

Equipped with Sunway SW26010 processors, Sunway TaihuLight is the first supercomputer that reaches the peak performance of over 125 PFLOPS [4]. The Sunway processor adopts a many-core architecture with 4 Core Groups (CGs), each of which consists of a Management Processing Element (MPE) and 64 Computation Processing Elements (CPEs) [7]. There is a 64 KB manually-controlled Local Device Memory (LDM) on each CPE. The Sunway many-core architecture also provides DMA and register communication for efficient memory access and communication on CPEs.

In this paper, we propose an efficient GBDT implementation for the Sunway many-core processor, which is an attractive target for accelerating the performance of GBDT with its unique architectural designs. The hotspot of GBDT can be further divided into two parts: *1)* sorting all the feature values before computing the gains; *2)* computing gain for every possible split. To speedup the hotspot, we partition the data into finer granularities such as *blocks* and *tiles* to enable efficient data access on CPEs. To improve the performance of sorting, we divide CPEs into multiple roles for pipelining the computation of segmenting, sorting, and merging with better parallelism. We evaluate the optimized GBDT implementation *swGBDT* with representative datasets and demonstrate its superior performance compared to other implementations on Sunway.

Specifically, this paper makes the following contributions:

- We propose a memory access optimization mechanism, that partitions the data into different granularities such as *blocks* and *tiles*, in order to leverage LDM and register communication for efficient data access on CPEs.
- We propose an efficient sorting algorithm on Sunway by segmenting and sorting the data in parallel and then merging the sorted sequences. During the sorting and merging, we divide the CPEs into multiple roles for pipelining the computation.
- We implement *swGBDT* and evaluate its performance by comparing with the serial implementation on MPE and parallel XGBoost on CPEs using representative datasets. The experiment results show 4.6× and 2× speedup, respectively.

This paper is organized as follows. We give the brief introduction of GBDT algorithm and Sunway architecture as background in Sect. 2. Section 3 describes our design methodology for *swGBDT*. Section 4 shows the implementation details of *swGBDT*. In Sect. 5, we compare *swGBDT* with both serial GBDT implementation and parallel XGBoost on synthesized and real-world datasets in terms of performance. Related works are presented in Sect. 6 and we conclude our work in Sect. 7.

2   Background

2.1   Sunway Many-Core Processor

The Sunway SW26010 many-core processor is the primary unit in Sunway Tai-huLight supercomputer. The illustration of the many-core architecture within a single Core Group (CG) of SW26010 is in Fig. 1. There are four CGs in a single SW26010 processor. The peak double-precision performance of a CG can be up to 765 GFLOPS, while the theoretical memory bandwidth of that is 34.1 GB/s. Moreover, the CG is comprised of a Management Processing Element (MPE), 64 Computation Processing Elements (CPEs) in a 8×8 array and a main memory of 8 GB. The MPE is in charge of task scheduling whose structure is similar to mainstream processors, while CPEs are designed specifically for high computing output with 16 KB L1 instruction caches and 64 KB programmable Local Device Memories (LDMs). There are two methods for memory access from main memory in the CG to a LDM in the CPE: DMA and global load/store (*gld/gst*). DMA is of much higher bandwidth compared to *gld/gst* for contiguous memory access. The SW26010 architecture introduces efficient and reliable register communication mechanism for communication between CPEs within the same row or column which has even higher bandwidth than DMA.

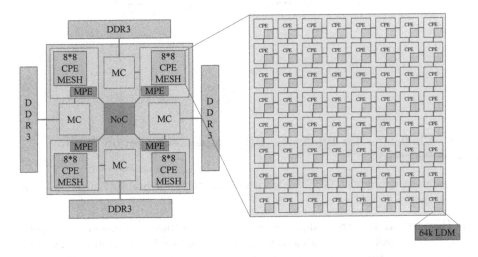

Fig. 1. The many-core architecture of a Sunway core group.

2.2   Gradient Boosted Decision Tree

The Gradient Boosted Decision Tree is developed by Friedman [6]. The pseudo-code of GBDT algorithm is presented in Algorithm 1 [20]. The training of GBDT involves values from multiple instances under different attributes and there are several hyperparameters in GBDT: the number of trees N, the maximum depth of tree d_{max} and the validation threshold of split points β. To store the dataset of GBDT algorithm, the sparse format [20] is developed to reduce the memory cost which only stores the non-zero values instead of values of all attributes in all instances as the dense format. We use the sparse format for $swGBDT$.

Moreover, as shown in Algorithm 1, GBDT trains the decision trees iteratively using the residual errors when the loss function is set to mean squared error. During each iteration, in order to find the best split points which is the bottleneck of GBDT, the algorithm needs to search for the maximum gain in one attribute, which will generate a preliminary split point that is appended to set P, and finally the best split point will be extracted from the set P with a validation threshold constant β. Thus the primary process in searching for best split points are gain computation and sorting. The *gain* among all instances of one attribute can be derived from Eq. 1, where G_L and G_R are the sum of first-order derivatives of loss function in left or right node respectively, while H_L and H_R are the sum of second-order derivatives of loss function in left or right node, respectively. The first-order and second-order derivatives can be computed from Eq. 2 and Eq. 3 respectively, where E is the loss function and it is set to be mean squared error in $swGBDT$.

$$gain = \frac{1}{2}[\frac{G_L^2}{H_L + \lambda} + \frac{G_R^2}{H_R + \lambda} - \frac{(G_L + G_R)^2}{H_L + H_R - \lambda}] \tag{1}$$

$$g_i = \frac{\partial E}{\partial y_i} \tag{2}$$

$$h_i = \frac{\partial^2 E}{\partial y_i^2} \tag{3}$$

2.3   Challenges for Efficient GBDT Implementation on Sunway Processor

In order to implement GBDT algorithm efficiently on Sunway, there are two challenges to be addressed:

1. How to leverage the unique many-core architecture of Sunway to achieve effective acceleration. Unlike random forest that each tree is independent of each other, the computation of each tree in GBDT depends on the result of the previous tree, which prevents the tree-level parallelism. Therefore, we need to design a more fine-grained parallel scheme to fully utilize the CPEs for acceleration.
2. How to improve the efficiency of memory access during GBDT training. The large number of random memory accesses during GBDT training lead to massive *gld/gst* operations with high latency. The poor locality with random memory access deteriorates the performance of GBDT. Therefore, we need to design a better way to improve memory access efficiency.

Algorithm 1. GBDT Algorithm

1: Input: **I**, d_max, β, N
2: Output: **T**
3: **T** $\leftarrow \phi$
4: **for** $i = 1 \rightarrow N$ **do**
5:    $T_i \leftarrow$ Tree_Init(**T**)
6:    **P** $\leftarrow \phi$
7:    **N** $\leftarrow$ RootNode(T_i)
8:    **A** $\leftarrow$ GetAttribute(**I**)
9:    **for** $n \in$ **N** **do**
10:      **if** $d >$ GetDepth(n) **then**
11:        $\mathbf{I}_n \leftarrow$ GetInstance(n)
12:        **for** each $A \in$ **A** **do**
13:          $g_m \leftarrow 0$
14:          $\mathbf{V}_n \leftarrow$ GetAttributeValue(A, n)
15:          $(g_m, p) \leftarrow$ MaxGain($\mathbf{I}_n, \mathbf{V}_n, A$)
16:          $P \leftarrow$ GetNewSplit($P, (A, g_m, p)$)
17:        **end for**
18:        $(A*, g*_m, p*) \leftarrow 0$
19:        **for** each $(A, g_m, p) \in P$ **do**
20:          **if** $(g* < g$ and $g > \beta)$ **then**
21:            $(A*, g*_m, p*) \leftarrow (A, g_m, p)$
22:          **end if**
23:        **end for**
24:        **if** $g*_m = 0$ **then**
25:          RemoveLeafNode(n, **N**)
26:        **else**
27:          $(n_1, n_2) \leftarrow$ SplitNode($n, A*, p*$)
28:          UpdateLeaf(**N**, n_1, n_2)
29:        **end if**
30:      **end if**
31:    **end for**
32: **end for**

---

3 Methodology

3.1 Design Overview

In this paper, data partitioning and CPE division are used to reduce the time of memory access through prefetching. For data partition, as shown in Fig. 2, firstly, we divide the data into *blocks* evenly according to the number of CPEs participating in the computation. Then we divide the *blocks* into *tiles* according to the available space of every CPE's LDM. When calculating the data from a *tile*, the DMA is used to prefetch the next *tile*. That's how we use the double buffering to hide the data access delay. When multi-step memory access or multi-array access are simultaneously needed (such as computing $A[i] = B[i] + C[i]$ needs access array A, B and C simultaneously), we divide the CPEs into data cores called *loaders* and computing cores called *savers*. *Loaders* prefetch data and then send it to *savers* for calculating by register communication. Meanwhile, for the reason that sorting operation is the most time-consuming, we propose an efficient sorting method. Firstly, we divide the data to be sorted evenly into 64 segments and sort them separately by 64 CPEs to achieve the maximum speedup ratio. Then we merge the 64 segments by dividing the CPEs into different roles and levels and register communication. Every 128 bits transferred by register communication is divided into four 32-bit length part as shown in Fig. 3.

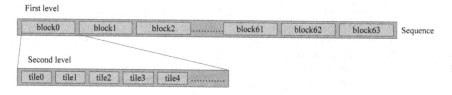

Fig. 2. The illustration of bistratal array blocking.

3.2   Data Prefetching on CPE

When there is a N-length big array named ARR participating in calculating, we firstly partition it into K *blocks* evenly (normally 64 when the CPE division in Sect. 3.1 is not needed, otherwise 32), so that every CPE processes a *block*. Because normally the processing time of every element in ARR is the same, so the static partition can achieve load balance. Then every CPE divides its *block* into *tiles* according to its usable LDM size. If the size of a *tile* is too small, more DMA transactions will be needed, whereas the size is too large, the *tile* will not be able to fit the limit of LDM. As a result, we use the equation $T = \frac{M}{\sum_0^{n-1} Pi}$ to calculate the number of *tiles*, in which T denotes the number of *tiles*, M denotes the LDM usable space size, n denotes the number of arrays that participate in the task, P_i denotes the element size of every array. Because the DMA is an asynchronous operation, it needs no more computation after sending the request, so it can be paralleled with computations. Thus we use the double buffering to hide the DMA time. In the beginning, the CPE loads the first *tile* and sends the DMA request for prefetching the next *tile*, then begins calculating. Every time it finish the calculating of one *tile*, the next *tile* has been prefetched by DMA, so the CPE sends a new DMA transaction for the next uncached *tile* and begins calculating the cached *tile*. That's how our double-buffering works.

In the training process of GBDT, we will face computing tasks like $C[i] = func(A[B[i]])$ which need multi-step memory access. Due to the *gld* operation in the second step, the memory access is of high latency and low bandwidth. Meanwhile, all CPEs access memory at the same time will cause the load of memory controller too heavy. So, we use the CPE division mode at these times, set half of CPEs as data cores called *loader*, another half of CPEs as computing cores called *saver* because they also need to save the final result to the main memory. There is a one-to-one relationship between *saver* and *loader*. The multiple roles

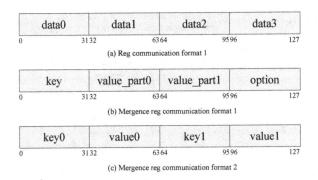

data0	data1	data2	data3
0 31 32	63 64	95 96	127

(a) Reg communication format 1

key	value_part0	value_part1	option
0 31 32	63 64	95 96	127

(b) Mergence reg communication format 1

key0	value0	key1	value1
0 31 32	63 64	95 96	127

(c) Mergence reg communication format 2

Fig. 3. The message formats used in register communication.

of CPEs and data communication are shown in Fig. 4. The *loader* firstly uses the data partitioning to prefetch *tiles* from array B, then uses the *gld* to get the value of $A[B[i]]$, finally sends it to its *saver* by register communication. We use the communication format in Fig. 3(a). The *saver* computes the $C[i]$ and saves $C[i]$ into the buffer and saves the result to the main memory by a DMA request when fills a buffer.

3.3   Sort and Merge

The sorting of large array is the main hotspot. To make full use of the 64 CPEs and to maximize parallelism, we firstly divide the array evenly into 64 segments, every CPE sorts a segment so that we can get 64 sorted sequences $A_0, A_1, A_2, \ldots, A_{63}$, then we merge them to get the final result. As shown in Fig. 5, each round carries out two combined mergence, 32 sorted sequences are got after the first round, 16 after the second round and so on, 6 rounds are needed to get the final result. For the reason that unmerged data may be replaced, as shown in Fig. 6, during every merging round, the data source and destination must be different. This means that at least two times of memory reading and writing is needed, reading from source and writing to a temporary location then reading from the temporary location and writing to the source. If we do not implement the data reusage through register communication, each round of merging requires a time of memory reading and memory writing, that are reading data for merging and writing the result into memory. 6 times of data reading and writing is needed for 6 rounds of mergence. This will lead to a large amount of data movements which will cause unnecessary time consumption. In this paper, we divide the CPEs into different roles and levels and use register communication to reduce the times of memory reading and writing from six to two. To achieve this goal, the 6 rounds of mergence is divided into two steps. The first step only includes the first round of mergence, writes the merged data into a temporary location. The second step includes all the last 5 rounds of mergence and writes the final result back to source location. Because the CPEs

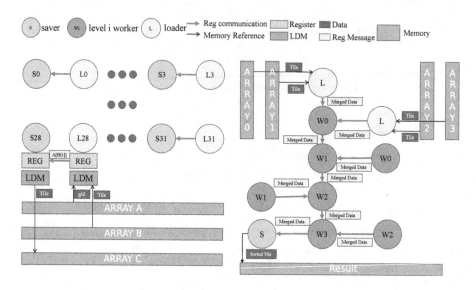

Fig. 4. The multiple roles of CPEs and data communication.

are divided into different roles and levels and compose a pipeline, the merging results of intermediate rounds are all transmitted by register communication to CPEs that doing the next rounds' mergence instead of writing back to memory, thus only one round of memory reading and writing is needed. The formats of Fig. 3(b) and (c) are used for register communication.

In the first step, the CPEs are divided into two types, *loaders* and *savers*. Each *loader* corresponds to a *saver*, they are in the same row so that register communication can be directly performed. Every *loader* reads two sequences with prefetching method mentioned in Sect. 3.1. Then *loaders* send the merged data to its *saver* through register communication. The roles and data stream are similar to the left part of Fig. 4, the difference is that in mergence, no *gld* is needed and all the data is got by DMA. For the fact that the key of all the data we will sort is non-negative integers, *loaders* send a message to its *saver* with the key field set to −1 as the flag of data transmitting ended after all the data is got and merged and sent to its *saver*. Each *saver* holds a double buffer, it saves the data into its buffer every time it receives data from its *loader*. When one part of its double buffer is full, it will write the data back to memory by a DMA request and use another part of the double buffer for data receiving. When *savers* receive the data with the value of the key field is −1 which means the data transmitting is ended, they will write all the remaining data in their double buffer back to memory and end working.

In the second step, the CPEs are divided into three types, *loaders*, *savers* and *workers*. A part of CPEs' hierarchical topology, division and data stream are shown in the right part of Fig. 4. *Workers* are set to be in different levels

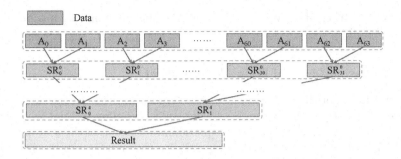

Fig. 5. The illustration of sequence merging.

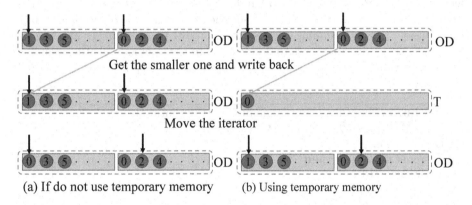

(a) If do not use temporary memory   (b) Using temporary memory

Fig. 6. The illustration of read-write conflict. (OD denotes the original data and T denotes the temporary memory)

according to the flow of the data stream, the *workers* that directly receive data from *loaders* are in the lowest level, the *worker* that directly sends data to the *saver* is in the highest level and the level of the others are sequentially increased according to the flow of the data stream. In Fig. 4, W_n means the level n *worker*. *Loaders* read data of two different sequences from memory and merge them and then send to the *workers* in the lowest level through register communication. The *workers* of every level receive data from two different lower-level *worker* and send the data to a higher-level *worker* after mergence through register communication. There is only one highest level *worker*. It sends the merged data to the *saver* instead of other *workers*. The *saver* saves the result back to memory. Also we set key of communication to -1 as the end flag.

4   Implementation

In this section, we present the implementation details of *swGBDT*, especially focusing on the gain computation and sorting process which are the major hotspots of GBDT. Moreover, we also describe the communication scheme for CPEs in detail.

4.1   Processing Logic of Gain Computation

As shown in Algorithm 2, to find the best gains, we need to consider every possible split and compute the gain of every split according to Eq. 1 to find the best gains. As the G_L and G_R in the equation are the sum of the g of instances on the left side and the right side, respectively. H_L and H_R are the same but the sum of h. The computation of g and h are shown in Eq. 2 and 3. Naturally, every feature value is a possible split point, but not all the instances have all the features. So, there are two ways to handle those instances that do not have the feature that the split uses. One is to divide the instances without this feature into the left side, that is assuming the feature values of these instances are smaller than the split point. Another is to divide them to the right side, that is assuming the feature values of these instances are bigger than the split point.

Algorithm 2. The Processing Logic of Gain Computation

1: Input: **S**, $fatherGH$, $missingGH$, $prefixSumGH$, λ
2: Output: $Gain$
3: **if** $thread\_id\%2 == 0$ **then**
4:     **for** each $split \in$ **S** **do**
5:         REG_GET(reg)
6:         $(f\_gh, m\_gh) \leftarrow reg$
7:         $r\_gh \leftarrow prefixSumGH[split]$
8:         $(l\_gain, r\_gain) \leftarrow$ ComputeTwoGain($f\_gh, r\_gh, m\_gh, \lambda$)
9:         **if** $l\_gain > r\_gain$ **then**
10:             $Gain[split] \leftarrow l\_gain$
11:         **else**
12:             $Gain[split] \leftarrow -r\_gain$
13:         **end if**
14:     **end for**
15: **else**
16:     **for** each $split \in$ **S** **do**
17:         $reg \leftarrow (fatherGH[split], missingGH[split])$
18:         REG_SEND($reg, thread\_id - 1$)
19:     **end for**
20: **end if**

Through the prefix sum operation, we already know the sum of g/h of the instance with the feature the split uses for all the possible split. The sum of g/h of the missing instances has been calculated, too. Thus we can easily calculate the G_L and G_R of two kinds of division by simple addition. The sum of g/h of the father node which is the sum of g/h of all the instances is also known as the result of the previous iteration. Thus we can get the G_L and H_L with a simple subtraction. So, they are all used as the input of the algorithm. In the algorithm, we obtain the index of the node that is to be split at first and get *father_gh* value with the index. Then we calculate the *gain* of missing instances on the left and right side, respectively. We only need the larger one and keep the original value if they are on the left or take the opposite if they are on the right. Since getting the *fatherGH* and *missingGH* are both two-step memory access, we cannot predict the memory access location of the second step because it depends on the result of the first step, so the data cannot be load into LDM by DMA easily. This means *gld* with high latency is needed. To reduce the performance loss, we divide the CPEs into *loaders* and *savers*. *Loaders* load the possible split into LDM using DMA and then get the *fatherGH* and *missingGH* with *gld*. Finally they send the data to their *saver* with register communication. *Savers* receive data, then compute the gains and write back to memory using DMA.

4.2   Processing Logic of Sorting

For sorting, we need to split the whole sequence to be sorted evenly into $A_0, A_1, A_2, \ldots, A_{63}$, each element in the sequence consists of two parts: key and value. It's a key based radix sort. As the key is a 32-bit integer, the time complexity is $O(\lceil 32/r \rceil \times n)$, where r is the number of the bits of the base, that is, r bits are used for calculation at each round. It can be seen that the larger the r is, the lower the time complexity is. However, the rounding up operation leads to the result that when r is set to r_0 and is not the factor of 32, the time complexity is the same with r using a factor of 32 that is the closest to r_0 but smaller than r_0. The factors of 32 are 1, 2, 4, 8, 16, 32 and the capacity of LDM is 64 KB which can only accommodate up to 16386 32-bit integers. When r takes 16, $2^{16} = 65536$ buckets are needed, the LDM will be exceeded even if the capacity of each bucket is 1. That is to say, the r can only take 8, so four rounds are needed to finish sorting. Because every CPE sorts independently, only 64 internally ordered sequences, $B_0, B_1, \ldots, B_{63}$, are obtained after sorting. 64 sequences are unordered with each other. We need the merging operation to get the final result.

For merging, we use the loader-saver mode to divide the CPEs in the first step. For stable sorting, as shown in Algorithm 3, the ith *loader* reads the data from B_{2i} and B_{2i+1} and merges them. We can consider the two sequences as two queues, the queue with data from B_{2i} calls q_0, the queue with data from B_{2i+1} calls q_1. Reading a *tile* means the data in the *tile* enqueue the corresponding queue. Comparing the key of the elements of the two queues continually, only when the key of the head element of q_1 is smaller than that of q_0 or q_0 is empty with no more data to be enqueued, q_1 can dequeue the head element, otherwise q_0 dequeue the head element. The dequeued element is sent to the corresponding *saver* by register communication. *Saver* saves the received data into buffer and writes the data into the main memory every the buffer is filled.

Algorithm 3. The Processing Logic of the Loaders of Mergence

1: Input: *sequences, sendto, seg_id*
2: $readbuffer1 \leftarrow sequences[seg\_id[0]].tiles$
3: $readbuffer2 \leftarrow sequences[seg\_id[1]].tiles$
    /*refill from memory when readbuff is empty, the refill operation is skipped here*/
4: **while Not** (*readbuffer1.empty* **And** *readbuffer2.empty*) **do**
5:     send =min(*readbuffer1, readbuffer2*)
    /*get the min item from two buffers and remove it*/
    /*if any buffer is empty then directly get from one the other*/
6:     REG_SEND(*send, sendto*)
7: **end while**
8: REG_SEND(*END, sendto*)

In the second step, we use the loader-worker-saver mode to divide the CPEs. Because the receiver of register communication cannot know the sender, a send-flag in the message that indicates the sender is needed if there are more than one sender in the same row or the same column with receiver. But the message length is only 128 bits, the sum length of key and value is 64 bits. If sender-flag is added, we can only send a pair of data a time which lower the efficiency. Thus, we propose a method that each CPE receives data from only one same-row CPE and one same-column CPE. And for stable sort, we ensure that the data received from the same-column CPE is in the former sequence than which from the same-row CPE by a carefully designed communication method. More specifically, the ith *worker* in a level receives last-level's $(2i)^{th}$ intermediate result by register communication from the same-column CPE and the $(2i+1)^{th}$ from the same-row CPE and sends the merged data (the ith intermediate result of this level) to the $\lfloor i/2 \rfloor th$ CPE of the next level as shown in Algorithm 4. According to the

Algorithm 4. The Processing Logic of the Workers for Mergence

---
1: Input: *sendto*
2: No Input and Output
3: REG_GETC($col_r ecv$)
4: REG_GETR($row_r ecv$)
5: **while** $row\_recv! = END$ **And** $col\_recv! = END$ **do**
6:     (*send, whichmin*) = Min($col_r ecv, row_r ecv$)
    /*readcache contains two queues, get the smaller item from the front*/
    /*if one queue is empty then get the head item from the other one*/
7:     REG_SEND(*send, sendto*)
8:     **if** *whichmin* == 0 **then**
9:         REG_GETC(*col_recv*)
10:    **else**
11:        REG_GETR(*row_recv*)
12:    **end if**
13: **end while**
14: REG_SEND(*END, sendto*)

---

design, when $i \bmod 2 = 0$, the data is sent to the same-column CPE, otherwise to the same-row CPE. Meanwhile, the read buffer of register communication is a queue with clear-after-reading, we do not need queues for merging. *Loaders* and *savers* work similar to the first step.

4.3 Synchronization Among CPEs

Since the CPE senders and receivers perform register communications according to the index of the array to be written or to be read and all the communications are one-to-one communications, no explicit synchronization mechanism is required. In other words, the whole 128 bits of the message are usable data. Therefore, our method can make full use of the bandwidth of register communication and thus improve communication performance.

5 Evaluation

5.1 Experiment Setup

Datasets. To evaluate the performance of our *swGBDT*, we use 6 datasets from LIBSVM Data [2] and 4 synthesized datasets named dataset1–4. The details of the datasets are shown in Table 1.

Table 1. The datasets for evaluation.

DataSet	Instances	Features	NNZ
dataset1	779,412	17,293	1,339,361
real-sim	72,309	20,958	3,709,083
news20	19,996	155,191	9,097,916
dataset2	7,245,157	179,232	12,445,475
dataset3	9,206,499	54,357	15,821,051
e2006	16,087	150,360	19,971,015
YearPredictionMSD	463,715	90	41,734,350
rcv1.test	677,399	47,236	49,556,258
dataset4	31,354,632	447,882	53,868,233
SUSY	5,000,000	18	88,938,127

Evaluation Criteria. We conduct our experiments on a CG of Sunway SW26010 processor. We compare the performance of our *swGBDT* with serial implementation on MPE and parallel XGBoost [3] on CPEs. The serial implementation is the naive implementation of our GBDT algorithm without using CPEs. We port the popular open source implementation[1] of XGBoost for parallel

---

[1] https://github.com/dmlc/xgboost.

execution on CPEs (with LDM used for better performance). In our experiments, we set the parameter depth to 6 and the number of trees to 40. All experiments run in single precision.

5.2   Performance Analysis

We use the average training time of a tree for comparison and use the MPE version as baseline. The results are shown in Fig. 7, Fig. 8 and Table 2, we can see clearly that *swGBDT* is the best one on all datasets. Compared to the MPE version, *swGBDT* can reach an average speedup of 4.6× and 6.07× for maximum on SUSY. Meanwhile, compared to XGBoost, we can achieve 2× speedup for average, 2.7× speedup for maximum. The advantage of *swGBDT* comes from the CPEs division that reduces the memory access time.

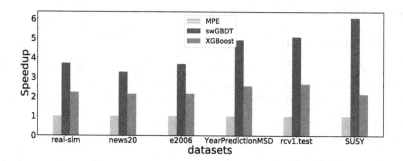

Fig. 7. The performance of *swGBDT* and XGBoost on real-world datasets

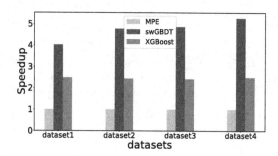

Fig. 8. The performance of *swGBDT* and XGBoost on synthesized datasets

Table 2. The training results for *swGBDT* and XGBoost.

DataSet	Training RMSE	
Name	*swGBDT*	XGBoost
dataset1	576	577
real-sim	0.47	0.5
news20	0.48	0.52
dataset2	575	577
dataset3	575	577
e2006	0.23	0.24
YearPredictionMSD	8.8	8.9
rcv1.test	0.43	0.43
dataset4	564	577
SUSY	0.37	0.37

5.3 Roofline Model

In order to analyse the efficiency of our implementation, we apply the roofline model [22] to *swGBDT* on a CG of Sunway processor. Giving a dataset with m instances and n features, assuming the non-zero numbers is nnz, we store it in CSC format. N_split is the number of possible splits during every training round. Let Q, W and I represent the amount of data accessed from memory, the number of floating point operations and the arithmetic intensity [23] respectively. The calculation of Q, W, I is shown in Eq. 5, 4, 6 respectively.

$$W = 19.5 * nnz + 37 * n\_split \tag{4}$$

$$Q = 22 * nnz + 32.5 * n\_split \tag{5}$$

$$I = \frac{W}{Q * 8bytes} = 0.125 + \frac{1.8 * n\_split - nnz}{70.4 * nnz + 104 * n\_split} \tag{6}$$

In our experiments, in most of the dataset, the n_split is about 0.9 of nnz. In this situation, $I = 0.1288$, the ridge point of Sunway processor is 8.46, we can see that the bottleneck of GBDT is memory access. The version without memory access optimization (the MPE version) gets the $I = 0.108$. Our optimization increases the arithmetic intensity for about 20%.

5.4 Scalability

To achieve better scalability, we divide the features into n segments evenly when the number of CGs is n. The ith CG only stores and processes the ith feature segment. Each CG computes its 2^{depth} splits and then determines the 2^{depth} best splits for all, where $depth$ is the depth of the tree currently. As shown in Fig. 9, we use up to 4 CGs on a processor for evaluating the scalability of *swGBDT*. Comparing to one CG, we can reach an average of 8×, 11.5× and 13× speedup when scaling to 2, 3 and 4 CGs, respectively.

6   Related Work

6.1   Acceleration for Gradient Boosted Decision Tree

To improve the performance of the GBDT algorithm, on one hand, some of the recent researches have been making efforts to modify the GBDT algorithm for acceleration. LightGBM [9] accelerate the time-consuming gain estimation process by eliminating instances with small gradients and wrapping commonly exclusive features, which can reduce computation. Later, Biau *et al.* [1] optimize the GBDT through combining Nesterov's accelerated descent [15] for parameter update. On the other hand, researches have been trying to transfer the GBDT to novel accelerators like GPU. Mitchell and Frank [14] implement the tree construction within GBDT algorithm in XGBoost [3] to GPU entirely to reach higher performance. Besides, Wen *et al.* [20] develop *GPU-GBDT* which enhance the performance of GBDT through dynamic allocation, data reusage and Run-length Encoding compression. The *GPU-GBDT* is further optimized to ThunderGBM [21] on multiple GPUs which incorporates new techniques like efficient search for attribute ID and approximate split points. However, those implementations do not target at Sunway architecture and there have not been any efficient GBDT algorithm designed to leverage the unique architecture features on Sunway to achieve better performance.

6.2   Machine Learning on Sunway Architecture

There have been many machine learning applications designed for Sunway architecture since its appearance. Most of the previous researches focus on optimizing neural networks on Sunway. Fang *et al.* [5] implement convolutional neural networks (CNNs) on SW26010 which is named swDNN through systematic optimization on loop organization, blocking mechanism, communication and instruction pipelines. Later, Li *et al.* [10] introduce swCaffe which is based on the popular CNN framework Caffe and develop topology-aware optimization for synchronization and I/O. Liu *et al.* [13] propose an end-to-end deep learning compiler on Sunway that supports ahead-of-time code generation and optimizes the tensor computation automatically.

Moreover, researchers have paid attention to optimize the numerical algorithms which are kernels in machine learning applications on Sunway architecture. Liu *et al.* [12] adopt multi-role assignment scheme on CPEs, hierarchical partitioning strategy on matrices as well as CPE cooperation scheme through register communication to optimize the Sparse Matrix-Vector Multiplication (SpMV) algorithm. The multi-role assignment and CPE communication schemes are also utilized by Li *et al.* [11] who develop an efficient Sparse triangular solver (SpTRSV) for Sunway. What's more, Wang *et al.* [19] improve the performance of SpTRSV on Sunway architecture through Producer-Consumer pairing strategy and novel Sparse Level Tile layout. Those researches provide us the inspiration of accelerating GBDT algorithm for Sunway architecture.

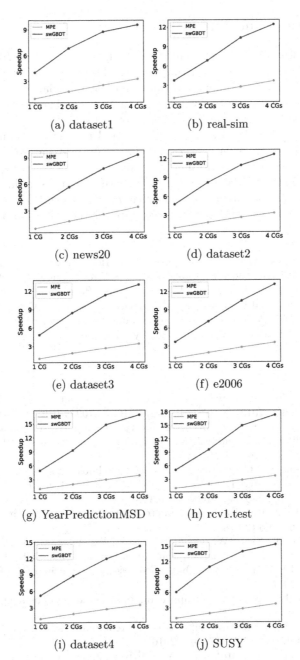

Fig. 9. The scalability of *swGBDT*.

7   Conclusion and Future Work

In this paper, we present an efficient GBDT implementation *swGBDT* on Sunway processor. We propose a partitioning method that partitions CPEs into multiple roles and partitions input data into different granularities such as *blocks* and *tiles* for achieving better parallelism on Sunway. The above partitioning scheme can also mitigate the high latency of random memory access through data prefetching on CPEs by utilizing DMA and register communication. The experiment results on both synthesized and real-world datasets demonstrate *swGBDT* achieves better performance compared to the serial implementation on MPE and parallel XGBoost on CPEs, with the average speedup of 4.6× and 2× respectively. In the future, we would like to extend *swGBDT* to run on CGs across multiple Sunway nodes in order to support the computation demand of GBDT at even larger scales.

Acknowledgments. This work is supported by National Key R&D Program of China (Grant No. 2016YFB1000304), National Natural Science Foundation of China (Grant No. 61502019, 91746119, 61672312), the Open Project Program of the State Key Laboratory of Mathematical Engineering and Advanced Computing (Grant No. 2019A12) and Center for High Performance Computing and System Simulation, Pilot National Laboratory for Marine Science and Technology (Qingdao).

References

1. Biau, G., Cadre, B., Rouvière, L.: Accelerated gradient boosting. Mach. Learn. **108**(6), 971–992 (2019). https://doi.org/10.1007/s10994-019-05787-1
2. Chang, C.C., Lin, C.J.: LIBSVM: a library for support vector machines. ACM Trans. Intell. Syst. Technol. **2**, 27:1–27:27 (2011). Software available at http://www.csie.ntu.edu.tw/~cjlin/libsvm
3. Chen, T., Guestrin, C.: XGBoost: a scalable tree boosting system. In: Proceedings of the 22nd ACM SIGKDD International Conference on Knowledge Discovery and Data Mining, pp. 785–794. ACM (2016)
4. Dongarra, J.: Sunway TaihuLight supercomputer makes its appearance. Nat. Sci. Rev. **3**(3), 265–266 (2016)
5. Fang, J., Fu, H., Zhao, W., Chen, B., Zheng, W., Yang, G.: swDNN: a library for accelerating deep learning applications on sunway TaihuLight. In: 2017 IEEE International Parallel and Distributed Processing Symposium (IPDPS), pp. 615–624. IEEE (2017)
6. Friedman, J.H.: Greedy function approximation: a gradient boosting machine. Ann. Stat. **29**, 1189–1232 (2001)
7. Fu, H., et al.: The sunway TaihuLight supercomputer: system and applications. Sci. China Inf. Sci. **59**(7), 072001 (2016)
8. Hu, J., Min, J.: Automated detection of driver fatigue based on eeg signals using gradient boosting decision tree model. Cogn. Neurodyn. **12**(4), 431–440 (2018)
9. Ke, G., et al.: LightGBM: a highly efficient gradient boosting decision tree. In: Advances in Neural Information Processing Systems, pp. 3146–3154 (2017)
10. Li, L., et al.: swCaffe: a parallel framework for accelerating deep learning applications on sunway TaihuLight. In: 2018 IEEE International Conference on Cluster Computing (CLUSTER), pp. 413–422. IEEE (2018)

11. Li, M., Liu, Y., Yang, H., Luan, Z., Qian, D.: Multi-role SpTRSV on sunway many-core architecture. In: 2018 IEEE 20th International Conference on High Performance Computing and Communications, IEEE 16th International Conference on Smart City, IEEE 4th International Conference on Data Science and Systems (HPCC/SmartCity/DSS), pp. 594–601. IEEE (2018)

12. Liu, C., Xie, B., Liu, X., Xue, W., Yang, H., Liu, X.: Towards efficient SpMV on sunway manycore architectures. In: Proceedings of the 2018 International Conference on Supercomputing, pp. 363–373. ACM (2018)

13. Liu, C., Yang, H., Sun, R., Luan, Z., Qian, D.: swTVM: exploring the automated compilation for deep learning on sunway architecture. arXiv preprint arXiv:1904.07404 (2019)

14. Mitchell, R., Frank, E.: Accelerating the XGBoost algorithm using GPU computing. PeerJ Comput. Sci. **3**, e127 (2017)

15. Nesterov, Y.: A method of solving a convex programming problem with convergence rate $o\left(\frac{1}{k^2}\right)$. Soviet Math. Dokl. **27**, 372–376 (1983)

16. Nowozin, S., Rother, C., Bagon, S., Sharp, T., Yao, B., Kohli, P.: Decision tree fields: an efficient non-parametric random field model for image labeling. In: Criminisi, A., Shotton, J. (eds.) Decision Forests for Computer Vision and Medical Image Analysis. ACVPR, pp. 295–309. Springer, London (2013). https://doi.org/10.1007/978-1-4471-4929-3_20

17. Prokhorenkova, L., Gusev, G., Vorobev, A., Dorogush, A.V., Gulin, A.: CatBoost: unbiased boosting with categorical features. In: Advances in Neural Information Processing Systems, pp. 6638–6648 (2018)

18. Roe, B.P., Yang, H.J., Zhu, J., Liu, Y., Stancu, I., McGregor, G.: Boosted decision trees as an alternative to artificial neural networks for particle identification. Nucl. Instrum. Methods Phys. Res. Sect. A: Accel. Spectrom. Detectors Assoc. Equip. **543**(2–3), 577–584 (2005)

19. Wang, X., Liu, W., Xue, W., Wu, L.: swSpTRSV: a fast sparse triangular solve with sparse level tile layout on sunway architectures. In: ACM SIGPLAN Notices, vol. 53, pp. 338–353. ACM (2018)

20. Wen, Z., He, B., Kotagiri, R., Lu, S., Shi, J.: Efficient gradient boosted decision tree training on GPUs. In: 2018 IEEE International Parallel and Distributed Processing Symposium (IPDPS), pp. 234–243. IEEE (2018)

21. Wen, Z., Shi, J., He, B., Chen, J., Ramamohanarao, K., Li, Q.: Exploiting GPUs for efficient gradient boosting decision tree training. IEEE Trans. Parallel Distrib. Syst. **30**, 2706–2717 (2019)

22. Williams, S., Waterman, A., Patterson, D.: Roofline: an insightful visual performance model for multicore architectures. Commun. ACM **52**(4), 65–76 (2009)

23. Xu, Z., Lin, J., Matsuoka, S.: Benchmarking sw26010 many-core processor. In: 2017 IEEE International Parallel and Distributed Processing Symposium Workshops (IPDPSW), pp. 743–752. IEEE (2017)

24. Xuan, P., Sun, C., Zhang, T., Ye, Y., Shen, T., Dong, Y.: Gradient boosting decision tree-based method for predicting interactions between target genes and drugs. Front. Genet. **10**, 459 (2019)

Numerical Simulations of Serrated Propellers to Reduce Noise

Wee-beng Tay[1](✉)⬤, Zhenbo Lu[1]⬤, Sai Sudha Ramesh[1]⬤,
and Boo-cheong Khoo[2]⬤

[1] Temasek Laboratories, National University of Singapore, T-Lab Building,
5A, Engineering Drive 1, #02-02, Singapore 117411, Singapore
tsltaywb@nus.edu.sg
[2] Department of Mechanical Engineering, National University of Singapore,
10 Kent Ridge Crescent, Singapore 119260, Singapore

Abstract. The objective of this research is to investigate the effect of serrations on quadcopter propeller blades on noise reduction through numerical simulations. Different types of the 5 inch 5030 propellers, such as the standard, modified and serrated, are tested. The modified propeller has a portion of its blade's trailing edge cut off to achieve the same surface area as that of the serrated blades to ensure a fairer comparison. Three-dimensional simulations propellers have been performed using an immersed boundary method (IBM) Navier–Stokes finite volume solver to obtain the velocity flow fields and pressure. An acoustic model, based on the well-known Ffowcs Williams-Hawkings (FW-H) formulation, is then used to predict the far field noise caused by the rotating blades of the propeller. Results show that due to the reduction in surface area of the propeller's blades, there is a drop in the thrust produced by modified and serrated propellers, compared to the standard one. However, comparing between the modified and serrated propellers with different wavelength, we found that certain wavelengths show a reduction in noise while maintaining similar thrust. This is because the serrations break up the larger vortices into smaller ones This shows that there is potential in using serrated propellers for noise reduction.

Keywords: Serrated trailing edge · Noise reduction · Propeller · Immersed boundary method

1 Introduction

Today, renewed attention is being focused on the first aeronautical propulsion device: the propeller. This is due to the increased use of unmanned air vehicles (UAVs), the growing market of general aviation, the increasing interest in ultralight categories or light sport air vehicles, and the growing importance of environmental issues that have led to the development of all-electric emissionless aircraft. One of the most popular small aircraft choices (weighing around 250-350 g) nowadays is the quadcopter, mostly in part due to its low cost, mechanical simplicity and versatile applications. However, one disturbing problem of propeller-driven aircrafts is their noise, which may

© The Author(s) 2020
D. K. Panda (Ed.): SCFA 2020, LNCS 12082, pp. 87–103, 2020.
https://doi.org/10.1007/978-3-030-48842-0_6

limit the aircraft's operation. This can be a serious concern if a UAV wishes to remain tactical, especially indoors since the audible noise level indoors is much lower.

Reducing propeller's noise can be achieved by a systematic or novel design of the propeller's geometry and aerodynamic characteristics. Most of the research work has been directed towards conventional engineering strategies to achieve good propeller designs. For instance, the performance of propellers can be improved by adjusting the number of blades, diameter, airfoil shape/distribution, chord, pitch distribution and coning angle [1]. Another method is through the use of contra-rotating propellers [2].

Alternatively, we can look to nature for inspirations. In contrast to conventional engineering strategies, studies on the application of bio-inspired features in propeller designs have been initiated recently [3–5]. One example is the owls, which developed serrated feathers on their wings and downy feathers on their legs that minimize aerodynamic noise, giving them silent flight. The serrations give the owl a better ability to control airflow, therefore allowing it to fly faster and achieve noise reduction at the same time. Another bio-inspired design is the porous trailing edge [6]. Ziehl-Abegg, Inc. primarily a ventilator company harnessed this feature by adding winglets to the blade tip and creating a serrated trailing edge on the rotor blades for achieving a quiet axial fan (FE2owlet axial fan). This resulted in a significant noise reduction up to 12dBA. However, due to the patent protection, only a few reference works related to this product can be found from the website. Thus, systematic research work for further developing a quiet UAV propeller system using this bio-propeller noise reduction concept is required.

The objectives of the present study are to preliminarily explore this bio-propeller concept using numerical modelling and further develop a low noise bio-propeller design strategy which can be used to optimize the propeller's blade geometry of the small (<20 cm) quadcopter. We will develop numerical models for calculating the aerodynamics and aero-acoustic performances of the propeller with focus on biomimetic serrated blades design using an in-house 3D Immersed Boundary Method (IBM) [7] Navier-Stokes solver, coupled with a Ffowcs Williams and Hawkings (FW-H) [8] acoustic code. A systematic analysis will be performed to improve the aero-acoustic performance of a bio-inspired propeller with a tentative goal of reducing its acoustic signature. Lastly, experimental validation will be performed to ensure that the numerical simulations have been performed accurately.

2 Numerical Setup

2.1 Aerodynamic Solver

For our simulations, an immersed-boundary method (IBM) [7] Navier-Stokes numerical solver [9] is used in this study. The reason for using an IBM based solver is because the blades of the propeller rotate. In some standard grid conforming numerical solvers which use the Arbitrary Lagrangian–Eulerian (ALE) [10] formulation, there is a need to constantly perform grid deformation or remeshing due to the blades' rotation.

This slows down the solver and affects the quality of the solution. A workaround is to enclose the propeller in a cylindrical domain and rotate that entire domain. However, there is also another problem with regards to the serrated propellers, as it is not trivial creating meshes in the vicinity of the serrations on the blades.

On the other hand, in IBM, the entire domain is composed of Cartesian grid and our bodies of interest are "immersed" in this grid, as shown in Fig. 1. To simulate the presence of the bodies, we need to add an additional forcing term fc to the momentum equation to give:

$$\frac{\partial u}{\partial t} = -u \cdot \nabla u + \frac{1}{Re}\nabla^2 u - \nabla p + fc, \tag{1}$$

where u is the velocity vector, t is the time, p is the pressure and Re is the Reynolds number. Equation (1) has been non-dimensionalized using the blade's velocity (U_{ref}, at distance of 75% from its root) and mean chord length (c) as the reference velocity and length respectively.

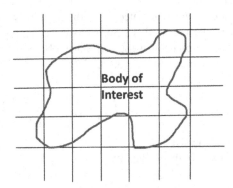

Fig. 1. Body of interest immersed inside Cartesian grid.

Out of the different variants of IBM, the discrete forcing approach is chosen because it is more suitable for our current Reynolds number (Re) of 31,407. This approach is based on a combination of the methods developed by Yang and Balaras [11], Kim et al. [12] and Liao et al. [13]. In the scheme, fc is provisionally calculated explicitly using the 1st order forward Euler and 2nd order Adams Bashforth (AB2) schemes for the viscous and convective terms, respectively, to give:

$$fc^{n+1} = \frac{u_f - u^n}{\Delta t} + \left(\frac{3}{2}\nabla.(uu)^n - \frac{1}{2}\nabla.(uu)^{n-1}\right) - \left(\frac{\nabla^2 u}{Re}\right)^n + \nabla p^n, \tag{2}$$

where n refers to the time step.

$$\nabla \cdot u = 0. \tag{3}$$

Equation (3) is the continuity equation. To solve the modified non-dimensionalized incompressible Navier-Stokes equations (Eq. (1) and Eq. (3)), the finite volume fractional step method, based on an improved projection method, is used. For the time integration, the second order AB2 and Crank Nicolson (CN2) discretization are used for the convective and viscous terms, respectively. For the spatial derivatives, the convective and viscous terms are discretized using the second order central differencing on a staggered grid. We solve Eq. (1) and (3) using the fractional step method as described by Kim and Choi [14], whereby the momentum equation is first solved to obtain a non-divergence free velocity field. Using this non-divergence free velocity, we solve the Poisson equation to obtain the pressure field, which in turn updates the velocity to be divergence free. The open source linear equation solvers PETSc [15] and HYPRE [16] are used to solve the momentum and Poisson equations respectively. At this relatively low Re of 31,407, no turbulence modelling is necessary because the flow is still largely laminar.

2.2 Force Calculations

Due to the fact that the body is not aligned with the Cartesian grid in the IBM, the forces acting on the bodies are calculated in a different way, as compared to the standard grid conforming solvers. In this case, we use the forcing term fc_{n+1} obtained earlier to calculate the non-dimensional force F_i on the body. More details about this method can be found in the paper by Lee et al. [15]:

$$F_i = -\int_{solid} fc_i^{n+1} dV + \int_{solid} \left(\frac{\partial u_i}{\partial t} + \frac{\partial u_i u_j}{\partial x_j} \right) dV, \tag{4}$$

where V is the volume of the wing.

The thrust coefficients c_t is then given by:

$$c_t = \frac{2c^2 F_t}{S}, \tag{5}$$

where V is the volume of the wing.

The thrust coefficients c_t is then given by:

$$c_t = \frac{2c^2 F_t}{S}, \tag{6}$$

where c and S refer to the reference wing mean chord length and wing surface area, respectively.

2.3 Solver Validation

The current IBM solver has been validated many times with different experiments. Some of the examples are:

1. Plunging wing placed in a water tunnel at a Re of 10,000 with an angle of attack of 20° [17]

2. Simultaneous sweeping and pitching motion of a hawkmoth-like wing in a water tunnel at a Re of 10,000 [18].

More details about the validation can be found in the paper by Tay et al. [9].

2.4   Acoustic Solver

We use a permeable form of FW-H equation, wherein the integration surface (a fictitious control surface) surrounds the non-linear flow region. This enables representation of the non-linear flow effects through the surface source terms in the equation [19]. The fictitious control surface onto which the CFD flow variables are projected, is assumed to be stationary. In the present study, the permeable control surface onto which the CFD flow variables (namely, pressure and velocity components) are projected, is assumed to be stationary. Hence, for a stationary control surface with negligible density fluctuations, the solution for acoustic pressure is given as follows:

$$4\pi p'(x,t) = \int_S \left[\frac{\rho_0 \dot{u}_n}{r}\right]_\tau dS(y) + \int_S \left[\frac{\dot{p}\hat{n}\cdot\hat{r}}{c_0 r}\right]_\tau dS(y) +$$
$$\int_S \left[\frac{p\hat{n}\cdot\hat{r}}{r^2}\right]_\tau dS(y) + \int_S \left[\frac{\rho_0 (u_n u_r)}{c_0 r}\right]_\tau dS(y) + \int_S \left[\frac{\rho_0 u_n u_r}{r^2}\right]_\tau dS(y)$$

(7)

where ρ_0 denotes the ambient fluid density; c_0 is the speed of sound; u_n denotes the dot product of the velocity vector with the unit normal vector $\hat{n}$; τ refers to the source time and t is the observer time given as $t = \tau + (r/c_0)$; y denotes the source location; r denotes the source observer distance. The subscripts n and r denote dot products with the unit vectors in the normal $\hat{n}$ and radiation $\hat{r}$ directions respectively. The Farassat 1A formulation has been used to transfer the time derivatives in the observer time into the surface integral terms in the FW-H equation, in order to prevent numerical instabilities. This results in a retarded-time formulation, which is solved using a mid-panel quadrature method and a source time-dominant algorithm [20]. Once the observer time pressure history is obtained, a fast Fourier transform (FFT) of the time series is performed to obtain the sound pressure level in frequency domain.

2.5   Simulation Setup and Grid Convergence Study

In this study, the reference velocity U_∞ is chosen as the tangential velocity 75% of the blade length from the propeller's root, which is calculated to be 44.77 m/s, with the blade length = 0.127 m and rotation speed = 9,000 rpm. The reference length is the average blade's chord length, which is 0.011 m. This gives a Re of 31,407. The reduced frequency is given as:

$$f_r = \frac{fc}{U_\infty} = 0.037,$$

(8)

where f and c are the frequency and chord length respectively.

Since the solver is IBM based, only Cartesian grids are used. The size of the computational domain is $24 \times 24 \times 25$ (in terms of non-dimensional chord length c)

in the *x*, *y* and *z*-directions respectively. The domain varies from -12 to 12, -12 to 12 and 0 to 25 in the *x*, *y* and *z*-directions respectively. The propeller is placed at the *x* = 0, *y* = 0, *z* = 6 location. Refinement is used in the region near the propeller and this region consists of uniform grid cells of length *dx*, which is the minimum grid length and it gives an indication of the resolution of the overall grid. We perform the simulations in quiescent flow, similar to the experimental setup.

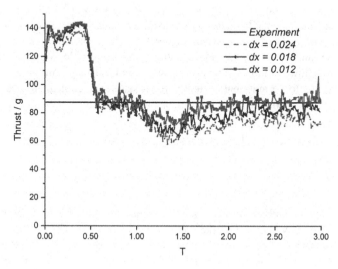

Fig. 2. Comparison of thrust with experiment and at *dx* = 0.024, 0.018 and 0.012.

Table 1. Average thrust obtained by experiment and at at *dx* = 0.024, 0.018 and 0.012

Avg thrust/g	Experiment	*dx* = 0.024	*dx* = 0.018	*dx* = 0.012
	87.5	75.2	82.1	89.1

Fig. 3. Isosurfaces plotted at Q criterion = 2 superimposed with pressure contour at time = 0.12T with *dx* = a) 0.024, b) 0.018 and c) 0.012.

For the grid convergence study, we perform simulations at $dx = 0.024c, 0.018c$ and $0.012c$, which translate to total grid sizes of $605 \times 605 \times 249, 792 \times 792 \times 307$ and $1161 \times 1161 \times 416$ respectively. Figure 2 shows the thrust at these resolutions, together with the average experimental result while Table 1 shows the average thrust obtained by experiment and simulations. The comparison between the experimental and numerical thrust improves as the grid resolution increases. Figure 3 shows iso-surfaces plotted at Q criterion = 2, superimposed with pressure contour at time = 0.12T for different grid resolutions. We observe that as resolution increases, the iso-surfaces increases due to having more number of grid cells. However, at $dx = 0.024$, there is much less isosurfaces as compared to $dx = 0.018$ and 0.012.

We next move on to the acoustic analysis at different grid resolutions. The sensitivity of CFD grid resolution on acoustic results has been studied for the baseline case. Further, the effect of different control surfaces on the overall sound pressure level has been studied to determine the use of appropriate permeable control surface for subsequent analyses of serrated propellers. Figure 4 shows two types of fictitious control surfaces namely, CS_0 (cylinder without end cap), CS_1 (cylinder with end caps) employed in the present study which are located at a distance of 1.1R (R is the radius of the propeller) from the centre of the propeller. Figure 5 shows the observer point locations at which the acoustic results will be monitored. The control surfaces are discretized into 42467 and 53044 triangular panels respectively, with finer discretization near the downstream end to enable accurate representation of acoustic sources, especially the contribution from tip vortices. The reason for studying the two surface types is to understand the effect of end caps (i.e. closure) on acoustic prediction. The use of open surface avoids wake penetrating the downstream end cap. The quadrupole source term in the porous FW-H equation has been neglected, since the control surface is assumed to reasonably contain the non-linear sound sources within it. Also, given that the propeller speed is subsonic, the effect of non-linear source terms is weaker in the far-field. However, they will be predominant when the observer point is located closer to the propeller axis of rotation, in the downstream end due to contributions from the tip vortices.

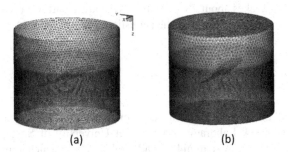

(a)   (b)

Fig. 4. Geometry and mesh of fictitious control surface located at 1.1 R from the center of propeller (a) CS_0 (b) CS_1.

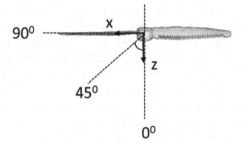

Fig. 5. Locations of observer points.

Table 2. Effect of CFD grid on acoustic results.

Control surface	Observer position	OASPL (dBA)		
		A (0.024)	B (0.018)	C (0.012)
CS_0	0^0	67.68	65.85	66.51
	30	67.85	66.44	66.54
	45	68.26	66.07	66.74
	60	68.15	65.86	66.25
	90	67.83	66.33	66.22
CS_1	0	70.77	71.18	72.11
	30	70.24	69.92	70.27
	45	70.13	70.12	69.68
	60	70.37	70.10	70.16
	90	69.38	69.54	69.06

From Table 2, it can be observed that grid B furnishes acoustic results that are closer to the fine grid resolution C. Hence, from these analyses, we decide that the minimum grid length of $0.018c$ will be used for all simulations in this study. Running a case for one period in parallel using 960 Intel(R) Xeon(R) CPU E5-2690 v3 @ 2.60 GHz processors takes about 70 h. As for the acoustic part, we used a maximum of 8 processors in parallel for computing the acoustic results at 8 observer locations which took about 4 h.

3 Experimental Setup

The acoustic and thrust measurements are conducted inside the anechoic chamber (located at the Temasek Laboratories@National University of Singapore). The propeller is mounted on the ATI mini40 Load Cell SI-20-1, which provides the thrust measurement, and the microphones are mounted at Points 1-5. The five points are aligned along a circle of radius, $R = 600$ mm, with Point 1 directly beneath the propeller and Point 5 directly above the propeller. The rest of the Points 2, 3 and 4 are spaced out equally along the circumference of the circle at 45° angle between each point as seen in Fig. 6. The acoustics and thrust measurements of the 5030 propeller will be taken at rotation speeds of 9000 rpm, for validation against the numerical data.

Fig. 6. Schematic of the experimental setup inside the anechoic chamber

The microphones (Brüel & Kjær Model 4953 ½ inch condenser microphone) are connected to a preamplifier and signal conditioner (Brüel & Kjær Model 2669, and NEXUS 2690-A, respectively). The analog signal of the microphone was sampled at f_s = 100 kHz by a fast analog-to-digital board (National Instruments PXI 6221). Each recording consists of 10^6 samples.

To avoid aliasing, a Butterworth filter was used to low-pass filter the signals at f_{LP} = 0.499 f_s - 1 (49,899 Hz). The corresponding power spectrograms were computed using a short-time Fourier transform providing a spectral resolution of about $0.1 Hz$. Using the microphone sensitivity and accounting for the amplifier gain setting, the voltage power spectrograms were converted to the power spectrograms of p'/p_{ref}, where p' is the fluctuating acoustic pressure and p_{ref} = 20µPa is the commonly used reference pressure. Converted to decibels and time averaged, these become sound pressure level spectra $SPL(f)$, where f is the measured frequency. An A-weighting correction was applied to the SPL spectra to account for the relative loudness perceived by the human ear. The corresponding overall sound pressure level (OASPL) is obtained by integrating the SPL spectra:

$$OASPL = 10 log_{10} \int_0^{f_{upper}} 10^{0.1 SPL(f)} df, \qquad (9)$$

where f_{upper} is the highest frequency of interest which in this study is $10 kHz$.

The thrust generated by the propeller is measured by an ATI mini40 load cell SI-20-1 whose force range and accuracy in the measured direction (Z direction) are 60 N

($\approx$6000 g) and $\pm$0.01 N ($\approx$1 g), respectively. The analog signal of the load cell was sampled at $f_s = 5$ kHz by a fast analog-to-digital board (National Instruments PXI 6221). Each recording consists of 5×10^4 samples, the recorded signal is filtered with a low-pass filter at $f_{LP} = 20$ Hz and then the mean value of the filtered data is calculated as the thrust of propeller. A tachometer is used to measure rotational speed of the propeller.

4   Methodology

The objectives of the present study are to preliminarily explore the serrated bio-propeller concept using numerical modelling and further develop a low noise bio-propeller design strategy which can be used to optimize the propeller's blade geometry of the small ($<$20 cm) quadcopter. The general steps of our methodology are:

1. Selection of a baseline propeller for our current study and measurement of its thrust and acoustic performance experimentally.
2. Use of our in-house numerical aerodynamic and acoustic solver to perform validation.
3. Re-design the propeller by adding serration to the its blades using CAD software and perform simulations to evaluate the performance of propellers with different serration parameters.

4.1   Initial Baseline Propeller Selection and Serrated, Cut-off Propeller Design

As mentioned earlier, our objective is to reduce the noise signature due to the propellers of small quadcopters weighing around 250-350 g. Hence, in this study, we have chosen the 5030 propeller as our baseline case. Each propeller can provide a thrust of around 80 to 90 g, rotating at 9000 rpm, and this give a total thrust of 320-360 g.

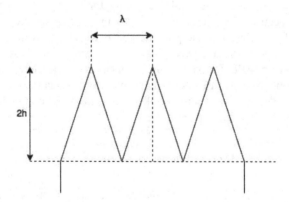

Fig. 7. Schematics of saw tooth serration parameters.

Next, we move on to the serrated propeller design. The saw tooth serrated design is represented in Fig. 7. The height of each saw tooth is = 2 h and the distance between each saw tooth peak is λ. In accordance with other references [21], the key parameter often used in literature is the ratio of λ/h. In this study, we fix h while varying the value of λ. The values λ/h selected are given in Table 3.

Table 3. Range of λ/h selected

λ/h	0.5	0.75	1	1.25	2

In the current design, part of the blade material is removed to create the serrations. This is different from the method used by some other studies [21], whereby the serrations are added onto the blades of the propeller. Due to the reduction in the surface area of the blades, it would not be fair to simply compare the baseline with the serrated propellers, even when using force coefficients which takes into account the surface area. Hence, a special type of propeller known as the cut-off propeller is created, as shown in Fig. 8. It has approximately the same surface area as the serrated propellers. One concern is that this modification changes the profile of the propeller's blade. However, this is inevitable because the adding of serrations modifies the propeller blade's profile as well. Hence, we will be comparing the serrated propellers with the baseline and cut-off propellers for a more comprehensive analysis.

Fig. 8. Frontal CAD view of the cut-off propeller.

5   Results and Discussions

5.1   Force Comparison

Figure 9 shows the thrust of the propellers over one period while Table 4 shows the average thrust. The experimental result is also given for comparison. Due to cost and time constraint, only two of the better performing serrated propellers have been 3D printed for validations.

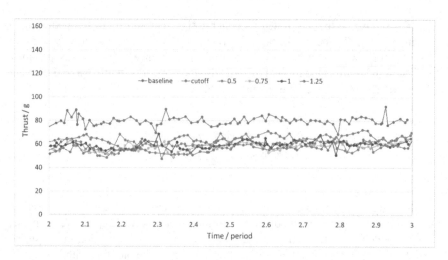

Fig. 9. Thrust generated by different propellers over one period.

Table 4. Surface area and average thrust generated by the different propellers

	Baseline	Cut-off	$\lambda/h = 0.5$	$\lambda/h = 0.75$	$\lambda/h = 1$	$\lambda/h = 1.25$
Surface area/cm^2	15.6	13.6	13.6	13.6	13.4	13.6
Average numerical thrust/g	80.4	67.4	65.6	61.6	62.5	59.5

Comparing between the surface area of the baseline and cut-off propellers, there is a 12.8% decrease in surface area. The serrated propellers have similar surface areas as the cut-off propeller. The average thrust of the cut-off propeller is 16.2% lower than that of the baseline case. Hence, the drop in thrust is higher than the surface area. However, we must also understand that the cut-off is simply a shortcut alternative to compare between serrated and unserrated propellers of similar area. It is not an aerodynamically ideal design and therefore will generate a lower than expected thrust. Moreover, thrust increase or decrease is usually exponential, instead of linear.

If we compare the cut-off propeller with the serrated ones, we observe that there can be a drop or increase in the thrust, although the surface areas of these propellers are similar. These vary from -2.7 to -11.7%.

5.2   Flow Visualizations

We now turned our attention to the comparison of the baseline, cut-off and serrated propellers. The $\lambda/h = 1$ serrated propeller is chosen since it gives the highest thrust. Similar to the previous comparison, there is only minor difference in the surface pressure distribution on the propellers. The key differences in this case lies in the vortex shedding at the trailing edge. As shown on the circled regions in Fig. 10, the serrated propeller tends to produce elongated, narrow and long vortices. It has been mentioned in some papers that the serration breaks up the larger vortices into smaller ones, and this in turn reduces the noise level of the propeller. This is because larger vortices are more energetic and they created larger pressure fluctuations during shedding.

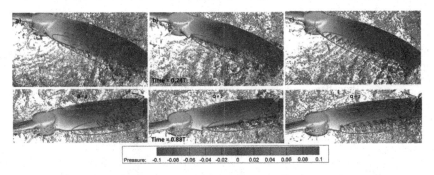

Fig. 10. Isosurface plotted at Q criterion of 2, superimposed with pressure contour of the a) baseline, b) cut-off and c) $\lambda/h = 1$ propellers at time = 0.24T and 0.88T. Circle regions denote differences.

5.3   Acoustic Analysis

We now present the results for propellers with various serrated trailing edge configurations. Table 5 presents the OASPL values at an observer distance of 10R from the propeller hub. In all the cases, the height of serration is fixed while the amplitude of serrations is varied to study the influence of trailing edge serrations on the acoustic field. Owing to computational time, the CFD results are extracted for one cycle after steady state convergence is achieved, followed by acoustic analysis. Figure 11 presents the plot of overall sound pressure level (dBA) for various serrated configurations at various observer locations. In general, the effect of including serrations at the trailing edge reduced noise level, especially in the vicinity of the downstream end. As evidenced in the isosurface plots in Fig. 10, the propeller with ($\lambda/h = 1$) reduces the intensity of trailing edge vortices compared to baseline and cut-off propeller configurations. As they are convected downstream, reduced noise levels are perceived near downstream observer locations. This is also reflected in OASPL plot in Fig. 11 and Table 5. However, the role of serrations in reducing noise levels are not effective for the in-plane observer point and its immediate vicinity. This supports the fact that dipole sources resulting from oscillating surface pressure distribution on the propeller are the main sources of noise at these locations. Furthermore, based on numerical investigations, there seems to be an optimal serrated configuration corresponding to ($\lambda/h = 1$) which can reduce downstream noise levels from 2.3 to nearly 5 dBA. Further numerical investigations will be conducted in future to substantiate the above fact. The amplitude and spacing of serrations play a crucial role in controlling the intensity of the shed vortices, especially those shed from the blunt roots of the serrations. This is possibly one of the reasons why the noise levels begin to increase beyond an optimal spacing of serrations [22, 23]. For instance, the noise levels begin to increase for $\lambda/h < 0.75$. Therefore, the effect of introducing serrations at the trailing edge eventually results in lower noise levels by enhancing the bypass transition to turbulence, compared to conventional transition to turbulence through laminar boundary layer.

Table 5. Comparison of OASPL values (dBA) at various locations for baseline and serrated 5030 propellers at 9000 rpm.

Propeller	Angle	CS_0	CS_1	Experiment
Baseline	0	65.85	71.18	67.17
	30	66.44	69.92	–
	45	66.07	70.12	67.68
	60	65.86	–	–
	90	66.33	–	65.21
Cut-off	0	67.78	71.23	68.49
	30	67.03	70.28	
	45	65.85	69.31	69.37
	60	65.05	–	
	90	65.71	–	66.36
SR – 1.25 (λ/h = 1.25)	0	66.92	68.73	
	30	67.20	70.30	
	45	66.60	70.54	
	60	66.43	–	
	90	65.30	–	
SR - 1 (λ/h = 1)	0	65.63	65.65	68.94
	30	67.12	66.52	
	45	67.57	67.56	67.33
	60	66.57	–	
	90	64.94	–	63.48
SR – 0.75 (λ/h = 0.75)	0	66.13	69.25	69.87
	30	65.79	68.65	
	45	66.54	68.39	67.42
	60	67.15	–	
	90	66.15	–	66.04
SR – 0.5 (λ/h = 0.5)	0	65.94	68.97	
	30	66.62	70.45	
	45	65.42	69.88	
	60	65.87	–	
	90	66.26	–	

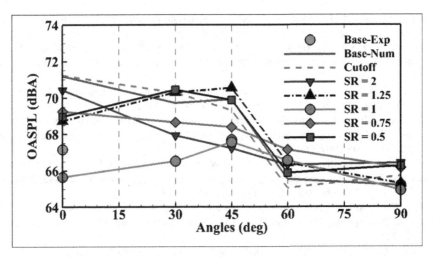

Fig. 11. Comparison of OASPL values for various propeller types.

6   Conclusions and Recommendations

Results show that when the serrated propellers are compared to the cut-off propeller, it is a decrease of 2.7% to 11.7%. There is a general trend of lower acoustic noise. The optimum case lies in the $\lambda/h = 1$ case, whereby while there is only a small change in the thrust, it can have up to 5 dB decrease in acoustic noise. These results demonstrated that serrations can be used to lower the noise level of propeller. More importantly, we have created a computational framework that links the numerical solver to the acoustic solver (based on FWH methodology) to study acoustic performance of propellers. This will be very useful for the systematic testing of future bio-mimetic propeller designs.

For the aero-acoustic part, the results show that the present solver can capture the tonal frequencies occurring at the harmonics of the blade passage frequency. The broadband components of the sound spectrum associated with small scale turbulent velocity fluctuations cannot be captured since the CFD solver is based on an incompressible flow averaged Navier Stokes equation.

References

1. Gur, O., Rosen, A.: Design of quiet propeller for an electric mini unmanned air vehicle. J. Propul. Power **25**, 717–728 (2009). https://doi.org/10.2514/1.38814
2. Sato, S.: Design and characterization of hover nano air vehicle (HNAV) propulsion system (2009). https://doi.org/10.2514/6.2009-3962
3. Agarwal, N.: Study of the unsteady aerodynamics associated with a cycloidally rotating blade (2017)
4. Clark, I.A., et al.: Bio-inspired canopies for the reduction of roughness noise. J. Sound Vib. **385**, 33–54 (2016). https://doi.org/10.1016/j.jsv.2016.08.027

5. Geyer, T., Sarradj, E., Fritzsche, C.: Nature-inspired porous airfoils for sound reduction. In: Tropea, C., Bleckmann, H. (eds.) Nature-Inspired Fluid Mechanics. NNFMMD, vol. 119, pp. 355–370. Springer, Heidelberg (2012). https://doi.org/10.1007/978-3-642-28302-4_21

6. Barone, M.F.: Survey of techniques for reduction of wind turbine blade trailing edge noise (2011)

7. Mittal, R., Iaccarino, G.: Immersed boundary methods. Annu. Rev. Fluid Mech. **37**, 239–261 (2005). https://doi.org/10.1146/annurev.fluid.37.061903.175743

8. Williams, J.E.F., Hawkings, D.L.: Sound generation by turbulence and surfaces in arbitrary motion. Philos. Trans. Roy. Soc. A Math. Phys. Eng. Sci. **264**, 321–342 (1969). https://doi.org/10.1098/rsta.1969.0031

9. Tay, W.B., Deng, S., van Oudheusden, B.W., Bijl, H.: Validation of immersed boundary method for the numerical simulation of flapping wing flight. Comput. Fluids **115**, 226–242 (2015). https://doi.org/10.1016/j.compfluid.2015.04.009

10. Hirt, C.W., Amsden, A.A., Cook, J.L.: An arbitrary lagrangian–eulerian computing method for all flow speeds. J. Comput. Phys. **135**, 203–216 (1997). https://doi.org/10.1006/jcph.1997.5702

11. Yang, J., Balaras, E.: An embedded-boundary formulation for large-eddy simulation of turbulent flows interacting with moving boundaries. J. Comput. Phys. **215**, 12–40 (2006). https://doi.org/10.1016/j.jcp.2005.10.035

12. Kim, J., Kim, D., Choi, H.: An immersed-boundary finite-volume method for simulations of flow in complex geometries. J. Comput. Phys. **171**, 132–150 (2001). https://doi.org/10.1006/jcph.2001.6778

13. Liao, C.-C., Chang, Y.-W., Lin, C.-A., McDonough, J.M.: Simulating flows with moving rigid boundary using immersed-boundary method. Comput. Fluids **39**, 152–167 (2010). https://doi.org/10.1016/j.compfluid.2009.07.011

14. Kim, D., Choi, H.: A second-order time-accurate finite volume method for unsteady incompressible flow on hybrid unstructured grids. J. Comput. Phys. **162**, 411–428 (2000). https://doi.org/10.1006/jcph.2000.6546

15. Balay, S., Gropp, W.D., McInnes, L.C., Smith, B.F.: Efficient management of parallelism in object oriented numerical software libraries. In: Arge, E., Bruaset, A.M., Langtangen, H. P. (eds.) Modern Software Tools in Scientific Computing, pp. 163–202 (1997). https://doi.org/10.1007/978-1-4612-1986-6_8

16. Falgout, R.D., Jones, J.E., Yang, U.M.: The design and implementation of hyper, a library of parallel high performance preconditioners. In: Bruaset, A.M., Tveito, A. (eds.) Numerical Solution of Partial Differential Equations on Parallel Computers, pp. 267–294. Springer, Heidelberg (2006). https://doi.org/10.1007/3-540-31619-1_8

17. Calderon, D.E., Wang, Z., Gursul, I.: Lift enhancement of a rectangular wing undergoing a small amplitude plunging motion. In: 48th AIAA Aerospace Sciences Meeting, Orlando, Florida, pp. 1–18 (2010)

18. Lua, K.B., Lim, T.T., Yeo, K.S.: Scaling of aerodynamic forces of three-dimensional flapping wings. AIAA J. **52**, 1095–1101 (2014). https://doi.org/10.2514/1.J052730

19. Brentner, K.S., Lyrintzis, A., Koutsavdis, E.K.: A Comparison of computational aeroacoustic prediction methods for transonic rotor noise. In: American Helicopter Society 52nd Annual Forum (1996)

20. Vieira, A., Lau, F., Mortágua, J.P., Cruz, L., Santos, R.: A new computational tool for noise prediction of rotating surfaces (fact) (2015). https://doi.org/10.5281/ZENODO.1099577

21. Ning, Z., Hu, H.: An Experimental study on the aerodynamic and aeroacoustic performances of a bio-inspired UAV propeller. In: 54th AIAA Aerospace Sciences Meeting, pp. 1–19 (2016). https://doi.org/10.2514/6.2017-3747

22. Parchen, R., Hoffmans, W., Gordner, A., Bran, K.A.: Reduction of airfoil self-noise at low mach number with a serrated trailing edge. In: International Congress on Sound and Vibration (1999)
23. Gruber, M.: Aerofoil noise reduction by edge treatments (2012)

High-Performance Computing in Maritime and Offshore Applications

Kie Hian Chua[✉], Harrif Santo, Yuting Jin, Hui Liang, Yun Zhi Law,
Gautham R. Ramesh, Lucas Yiew, Yingying Zheng, and Allan Ross Magee

Technology Centre for Offshore and Marine, Singapore (TCOMS),
Singapore, Singapore
chua_kie_hian@tcoms.sg

Abstract. The development of supercomputing technologies has
enabled a shift towards high-fidelity simulations that is used to com-
plement physical modelling. At the Technology Centre for Offshore
and Marine, Singapore (TCOMS), such simulations are used for high-
resolution investigations into particular aspects of fluid-structure interactions in order to better understand and thereby predict the generation
of important flow features or the complex hydrodynamic interactions
between components onboard ships and floating structures. In addition,
by building on the outputs of such simulations, data-driven models of
actual physical systems are being developed, which in turn can be used
as digital twins for real-time predictions of the behaviour and responses
when subjected to complex real-world environmental loads. In this paper,
examples of the high-resolution investigations, as well as the development
of digital twins, are described and discussed.

Keywords: Maritime and offshore · Digital twin · Deepwater ocean
basin · Autonomous vessel

1 Introduction

The maritime and offshore industries are transforming to improve efficiency,
safety and sustainability. With the advancement of sensing, computational and
communication technologies, engineers are now able to gain better insights into
how ships and offshore structures respond when subjected to environment loads.
This enables better risk management and reduces downtime. The ability to carry
out full-order simulations of fluid-structure interactions with higher fidelity, also
enables us to attain deeper insights into the complex flow processes that may be
present in scaled model tests. Concurrently, there is a push towards harnessing
data in order to evolve digital twins of physical systems that can be used for the

Supported by A*STAR, National Research Foundation and National Super Computing
Centre.

performance prediction of assets such as ships and offshore structures, as well as systems such as TCOMS' deepwater ocean basin (DOB) facility.

In this paper, the preliminary efforts using Harmonic Polynomial Cell (HPC) method to develop high-fidelity numerical models are described. The first example is to create a digital twin of the TCOMS' deepwater basin facility. The movement of wave paddles, the generated wave components, as well as the fully-nonlinear interaction between those wave components are modelled and simulated. High-fidelity simulations are carried out to investigate the potential onset of small-scale flow phenomena that may arise from the wave paddle mechanisms and the influence on the quality of generated waves. In the meantime, the application of parallel computations on evaluating the hydrodynamics of autonomous vessels is discussed. The objective is to develop a digital twin of the vessel for testing and implementing remotely-operated and autonomous navigation control systems and algorithms. The two series of work will be integrated into TCOMS' cyber-physical modelling framework later on, and to be coupled with physical model tests of marine structures. This is expected to generate new insights into the behaviour of marine systems in real operating environments.

2   Digital Twin of a Large-Scale Wave Basin

Ships and offshore structures need to be designed for high sea states where the predominant forcing is due to wave loading. Mooring line failures arising from large-amplitude slow drift motions, under-deck slamming due to vanishing air gap and wave-overtopping are possible scenarios that may require investigations. Due to their large displaced volume of offshore floating structures, the wave loads are dominated by inertial effects with viscous processes playing a secondary role. It is thus reasonable to use a physical wave basin facility to carry out scaled-down experiments based on Froude similarity to estimate the hydrodynamic loads and responses of these structures.

Within the context of the linear potential flow theory, the boundary element method (BEM) in frequency-domain has been widely applied, and it is the most efficient because the unknowns are only distributed over the mean wetted hull surface with the utilization of Green's identity. In the fully-nonlinear free-surface flow problems, however, the computational time and memory required by the BEM solving in time-domain increase strongly as the number of unknowns increases because the coefficient matrix for the unknowns is full. [11] argue that a field-solver based on the finite element method (FEM) is faster than the BEM for solving the wave-making problem because a sparse matrix is involved in the solution. The conventional BEM involves quadratic memory usage, $O(N^2)$, and requires $O(N^2)$ operations for an iterative solver or $O(N^3)$ operations if a direct method is used. Here, N is the number of unknowns; thus, large-scale storage and inefficient computation are considered bottleneck problems in the conventional BEM.

In order to enhance the investigation of the fore-mentioned hydrodynamic phenomena and facility better understanding of the underlying flow physics, a high-fidelity numerical wave tank has been developed to augment the physical deepwater ocean basin (DOB) in TCOMS. The numerical wave tank has the same dimensions ($60\,\mathrm{m} \times 48\,\mathrm{m} \times 12\,\mathrm{m}$) as the DOB and is similarly equipped with numerical representations of hinged-flap wave paddles on two sides. This allows us to simulate the wave generation, as well as the wave propagation across the domain of the DOB. A potential-flow based Harmonic Polynomial Cell (HPC) method, which is a numerical solver with accuracy higher than third order, is used [10].

A three-dimensional Cartesian coordinate system $Oxyz$ is defined with the Oxy plane coinciding with the undisturbed free surface and Oz axis orienting positively upwards. The fluid domain is discretised into overlapping hexahedral cells with 26 grid points. The velocity potential within each cell is represented as a linear combination of N harmonic polynomials:

$$\phi(X,Y,Z) = \sum_{j=1}^{N} b_j P_j(X,Y,Z) \tag{1}$$

where $P_j(X,Y,Z)$ with $j = 1, 2, \ldots, N$ mean harmonic polynomials associated with Legendre polynomials in a spherical coordinate system. Here, X, Y and Z are local coordinates relative to the stencil centre. Because the harmonic polynomials satisfy the Laplace equation naturally, there is no need to impose the Laplace equation. By imposing Eq. (1) on the 26 stencil points, one can obtain a linear equation system in the form of:

$$[A] \cdot \{b\} = \{\Phi\} \quad \text{with} \quad A_{i,j} = P_j(X,Y,Z), \; i = 1, 2, \ldots, 26 \tag{2}$$

Here, N is not necessarily equal to 26. If $N < 26$, the least square fitting can be used. By taking the inverse of Eq. (2), we can obtain the vector $\{b\}$:

$$b_j = \sum_{i=1}^{26} c_{i,j} \Phi_i \quad \text{with} \quad j = 1, \ldots, N, \tag{3}$$

where $c_{i,j}$ are elements of the matrix $[A]^{-1}$ or $\left[[A]^T \cdot [A]\right]^{-1} \cdot [A]^T$. Substituting Eq. (3) into Eq. (2) gives rise to:

$$\Phi(X,Y,Z) = \sum_{j=1}^{N} \left[\sum_{i=1}^{M} c_{i,j} \Phi_i\right] P_j(X,Y,Z) = \sum_{i=1}^{M} \left[\sum_{j=1}^{N} c_{j,i} P_j(X,Y,Z)\right] \Phi_i \tag{4}$$

Equation (4) indicates that the velocity potential at any point in the cell can be interpolated by the velocity potential on the surrounding nodes of the cell. By setting $x = 0$, $y = 0$ and $z = 0$, one can obtain the continuity equation at the stencil centre:

$$\Phi_{27} = \sum_{i=1}^{M} V_i \Phi_i \quad \text{with} \quad V_i = c_{1,i} \tag{5}$$

On the solid boundaries, the Neumann-type boundary condition requiring the derivative of the potential is implemented by directly taking the derivative of harmonic polynomials:

$$\nabla\Phi(X,Y,Z) = \sum_{i=1}^{M} U_i\Phi_i \text{ with } U_i = \sum_{j=1}^{N} c_{j,i}\nabla P_j(X,Y,Z) \tag{6}$$

The HPC method will yield a sparse coefficient matrix with a maximum band-width 27. On the solid boundaries, the Neumann-type boundary condition is satisfied. On the free surface, the kinematic and dynamic free-surface boundary conditions are satisfied:

$$\frac{\partial\mathcal{E}}{\partial t} + \frac{\partial\Phi}{\partial x}\frac{\partial\mathcal{E}}{\partial x} + \frac{\partial\Phi}{\partial y}\frac{\partial\mathcal{E}}{\partial y} - \frac{\partial\Phi}{\partial z} = 0 \text{ on } z = \mathcal{E}(x,y,t), \tag{7a}$$

$$\frac{\partial\Phi}{\partial t} + g\mathcal{E} + \frac{1}{2}\left[\left(\frac{\partial\Phi}{\partial x}\right)^2 + \left(\frac{\partial\Phi}{\partial y}\right)^2 + \left(\frac{\partial\Phi}{\partial z}\right)^2\right] = 0 \text{ on } z = \mathcal{E}(x,y,t) \tag{7b}$$

where $\mathcal{E}(x,y,t)$ represents the free-surface elevation.

In the time-domain HPC method, the Dirichlet-type condition is satisfied via prescribing the velocity potential and elevation on the free surface. A semi-Lagrangian scheme is used to track the free surface. The explicit fourth-order Runge-Kutta scheme is used to integrate the boundary conditions Eqs. (7a) and (7b) to update the potential and elevation of the free surface at each time step. To ensure stability, a Savitzky-Golay filter [9] is used to remove possible sawtooth waves.

In contrast to the industry-standard Computational Fluid Dynamics (CFD) solvers, such as Star-CCM+, Fluent and OpenFOAM, which solves the Navier-Stokes equations and the Poisson equation for pressure, there is only one unknown (velocity potential) on each node in the present HPC method compared to four unknowns (three velocity components and pressure) in the CFD solvers. Therefore, the present HPC solver is relatively efficient.

To give an example, Fig. 1 shows a snapshot of wave field with heading angle 45° for a rectangular wave basin with dimension of 30 m × 30 m × 4 m. The same numerical domain was used to investigate the physics of spurious waves generated by a row of wave paddles, for more details see [5]. In this numerical example, there are roughly 1.6×10^7 unknowns and the non-zero elements in the sparse matrix will be up to 4.24×10^8. In order to capture the important flow physics as much as possible, paddle movements are accounted for - this requires updating meshes attached to paddles at every time step.

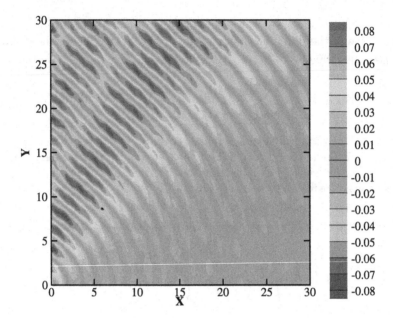

Fig. 1. Snapshot of wave field with heading angle 45°.

When numerically implementing the HPC method, the local coefficient matrix with dimension 26 × 26 was solved by the Linpack library, and the global sparse matrix was solved by the GMRES solver within Portable, Extensible Toolkit for Scientific Computation (PETSc) library [1]. The computation was conducted on the platform of National Supercomputing Centre (NSCC) with CPU of Intel(R) Xeon(R) CPU E5-2690 v3 @ 2.60 GHz, and a total of 5 nodes at 24 cores per node were used. It takes 23s to run each time step, and the efficiency is acceptable for the present application using the NSCC facilities. Nevertheless, the computational load for the numerical DOB is still non-trivial due to the large size of the domain being modelled. The method shows a great ability to resolve small scale wave features which are important to understand the remaining uncertainties inherent in the simulations.

3   Investigation of Gusset Effect in Between Wave Paddles

The DOB uses a dry-back wave paddle system, where gussets are used between the individual paddles to prevent water from entering the rear side of the paddles. Given that there will be a small amount of water trapped in the groove formed by the gusset, it is of interest to investigate whether there are any 'jetting' effects arising from the movement of the paddles as they generate waves, and whether there are higher harmonic wave components arising from the gap between paddles, which may affect the quality of the underlying generated waves.

CFD analysis is used to investigate this phenomenon and to quantify whether the ripples or 'jetting' effects could affect the shape of the underlying generated waves downstream of the wavemaker. Figure 2(a) shows the initial set up of two wave paddles and a layout of a gusset between two adjacent paddles and ripple strips. Figure 2(b) illustrates the shape and different parts of the gusset.

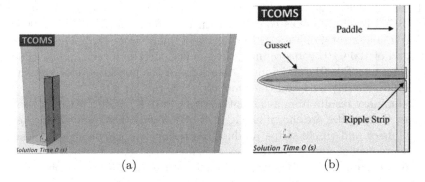

(a)   (b)

Fig. 2. (a) Initial set up of two paddles and a gusset/ripple strip layout between the adjacent paddles. (b) The shape and different parts of the gusset.

The gusset is modelled and simplified for CFD simulations. Bolts, nuts, washers and other joining mechanisms are removed and the geometry of the rubber bladder is modelled using a B-Spline curve to fit the manufacturer's requirements. The gap is intended to be as small as possible and there is an overlap in the ripple strip in the manufactured geometry. However, during operation, the forces acting on the flexible ripple strips create a gap due to the deformation.

In these simulations, the gap is modelled at a constant width of 5 mm. The wave paddles are modelled with mesh morphing using the B-Spline morphing method [4]. The paddle motion is generated using a first-order (linear) wave paddle signal.

The simulation solves Reynolds-Averaged Navier-Stokes equations by using the concept of a turbulent eddy viscosity prescribed by the Boussinesq approximation. This is achieved via $k - \omega$ SST model by solving the transport equations of turbulent kinetic energy, k and specific dissipation rate, ω [7]. The air-water interface is captured using a Volume of Fluid (VoF) method where the distribution of phases and the position of the interface are described by the fields of phase volume fraction. A high order interface capturing (HRIC) method is used to mimic the convective transport of immiscible fluid components such as air and water [8].

The computational requirements to simulate the gusset effects are extensive, due to the following considerations:

– Requirement of very fine mesh in and around the gusset and gaps to resolve the local flow features;
– Requirement of fine mesh at free surface to resolve the higher harmonic wave components;

– Requirement of moving mesh - rigid body motion to simulate paddle flapping motion; and
– High fidelity spatial and temporal discretisation.

For the cases presented in this paper, the mesh size for the computation is 14.4 million cells. The simulation was run on National Supercomputing Centre (NSCC) compute nodes equipped with Intel(R) Xeon(R) CPU E5-2690 v3 2.60 GHz, and a total of 5 nodes at 24 cores per node were used. This amounted to a total of 120 CPU cores running the simulation. The total compute time for each time step of 0.001 s and 5 inner iterations for the pressure–velocity coupling took approximately 3.6 s and the simulation was run for 30 s.

Preliminary results from a simulation of a row of 6 paddles with 5 gussets in between the paddles are shown in Fig. 3. It is observed that the combined effect of the gusset and ripple strips produce scattering (ripple) of higher harmonic wave components, similar to Huygens principle.

Closer examination of the higher harmonic wave components is conducted by looking at the simulated surface elevation (wave) - time series at several locations along the centreline of the computational domain. Figure 4 shows the results at three locations (0.05 m, 0.1 m and 0.7 m downstream of the wave paddles). It can be observed that the higher harmonic wave components decay rapidly within 0.7 m of advection along the tank. Therefore, it can be concluded that the presence of such higher harmonic waves do not alter the form of the underlying primary waves downstream of the wave paddles. It is important to note that high resolution computations are required to adequately resolve the fine flow details of interest. Therefore the capabilities afforded by NSCC are essential to achieve the outcome through adequate computational power.

4   Digital Twin of Marine Vessel for Remote and Autonomous Navigation

The maritime industry evolves quickly towards remotely controlled and autonomous vessels for more reliable and sustainable missions. This transformation is driven partly by the digitalisation trend, involving sensing, big data and deep learning analytics, and partly by the need to reduce the operating cost of manning a vessel. The marine autonomous surface vessel (MASS) technologies adopted as of this date are typically rely on situational awareness and predictive analytics methods in relatively calm sea-states. One of TCOMS' missions is to carry out further investigations and gain deeper understanding of MASS hydrodynamic response in challenging sea-states, essentially the manoeuvrability of vessels under the disturbance of wind, waves and currents. This enables the development of the hydrodynamic digital twin for smart vessels, in terms of providing accurate projection of their future states and therefore improves the effectiveness of steering actions, particularly for route planning and collision avoidance.

Fig. 3. Snapshot of a wavefield produced from a row of wave paddles.

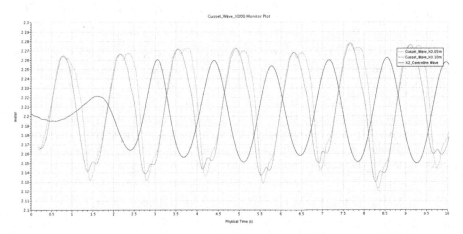

Fig. 4. Simulated surface elevation (or waves) - time series at three locations down-stream of the wave paddles (0.05 m, 0.1 m and 0.7 m) along the centreline of the computational domain.

In order to capture vessel's seakeeping and manoeuvring behavior, and the non-linear interactions between hull, propellers, rudder and environmental loads, we adopted the unsteady RANS-based CFD computations, applying the overset grid technique to solve for the fluid flow pressure distribution, resulting force and hence 6-DoF global motions of the vessel. The conservation equations of mass and momentum are discretised using the Finite Volume Method (FVM). Often, a significant number of grid points (6.0 M–15.0 M) is required to resolve the complex physical shape of ship hull and its appendages, as well as the sharp interface between water and air over a sufficiently large volume. Simulations as such can only be carried out by parallel computations with hundreds of CPUs under the MPI communication protocol, which are accessible from NSCC.

CFD computations carried out in this section share the common assumption of incompressible Newtonian fluid properties. The conservation equations for mass, momentum and energy are used in their integral form as the mathematical basis. The fluid is regarded as a continuum, which assumes that the matter is continuously distributed in space. The concept of continuum enables us to define velocity, pressure, temperature, density and other important quantities as continuous functions of space and time. When solving high Reynolds number problems, turbulence has to be considered, and to fully resolve the turbulent flow physics with Direct Numerical Simulations (DNS), grid size close to Kolmogorov scale (in micrometer) is necessary. However, this is considered to be unrealistic for ship hydrodynamic applications where the domain size is usually in hundreds of meters. Therefore, Reynolds-averaged Navier-Stokes (RANS) is introduced to simplify the calculation of turbulence quantities. The generic transport equation of the RANS model can be written in the following form [3],

$$\frac{\partial}{\partial t} \int_V \rho \phi dV + \oint_S \rho \phi \mathbf{v} \cdot \mathbf{ds} = \oint_S \Gamma_\phi \mathbf{grad}\phi \cdot \mathbf{ds} + \oint_S \mathbf{q}_{\phi S} \cdot \mathbf{ds} + \int_V q_{\phi V} dV \qquad (8)$$

where ϕ stands for the transported variable such as velocity potentials, Γ_ϕ is the diffusion coefficient and $q_{\phi S}$ and $q_{\phi V}$ stand for the surface exchange terms and volume sources, respectively. The momentum and energy equations can also be written in the discrete form to facilitate the numerical solution. The closure of the transport equation is by the $k - \omega$ SST turbulence model [7]. Terms in Eq. 8 can be replaced by the turbulence kinetic energy k and the specific dissipation rate ω in Table 1. Details of the closure coefficients and the auxiliary relations can be found in the above mentioned literature.

Table 1. k and ω equations in the RANS turbulence modelling

ϕ-equation	k-equation	ω-equation
Γ_ϕ	$\mu + \dfrac{\mu_t}{\sigma_\omega}$	$\mu + \dfrac{\mu_t}{\sigma_\omega}$
$\mathbf{q}_{\phi S}$	0	0
$\mathbf{q}_{\phi V}$	$\rho \tilde{P}_k - \rho\beta^* \omega k$	$\rho\dfrac{\gamma}{\nu_t}P_k - \rho\beta\omega^2 + \rho(1 - F_1)2\sigma_{\omega 2}\dfrac{1}{\omega}\dfrac{\partial k}{\partial x_j}\dfrac{\partial \omega}{\partial x_j}$

The FVM method of descretisation is applied to solve for the numerical solution of the transport equations. The solution domain is discretised by an unstructured mesh composed of a finite number of contiguous control volumes (CVs) or cells. Each control volume is bounded by a number of cell faces which compose the CV-surface and the computational points are placed at the center of each control volume. The discretisation of each particular term in Eq. 8 is summarised in Table 2.

It is noted the pressure does not feature in the continuity equation of incompressible fluid which therefore cannot be directly used as an equation for pressure. A possible way around this problem is to solve the momentum and continuity equations simultaneously in a coupled manner. The strategy adopted in most of our unsteady computations to resolve the pressure-velocity coupling is based on the PIMPLE algorithm, a combination of Pressure Implicit with Splitting of Operator (PISO) and Semi-Implicit Method for Pressure-Linked Equations (SIMPLE) [2]. The computation of pressure-velocity coupling normally takes a significant amount of CPU power especially for cases with large amount of grids.

Table 2. Discretisation schemes of individual term from the transport equation

Numerical term	Expression	Discretisation method
Rate of change	$\dfrac{\partial}{\partial t} \displaystyle\int_{\Delta V} \rho\phi dV$	Mid-point approximation
Convection	$\displaystyle\sum_{j=1}^{N} \oint_S \rho\phi\mathbf{v} \cdot \mathrm{ds}$	Blended Central differencing & Upwind differencing scheme
Diffusion	$\displaystyle\sum_{j=1}^{N} \oint_S \Gamma_\phi \mathbf{grad}\phi \cdot \mathrm{ds}$	Gauss's theorem & Mid-point approximation
Surface source	$\displaystyle\sum_{j=1}^{N} \oint_S \mathbf{q}_{\phi S} \cdot \mathrm{ds}$	Central differencing scheme
Volume source	$\displaystyle\sum_{j=1}^{N} \int_V q_{\phi V} dV$	Mid-point approximation

Computations carried out under this part of scope focus on evaluation of the manoeuvring and seakeeping performance of the MASS. One of the most computational intensive cases is to compute the free running dynamic manoeuvres under self-propelled conditions. The simulation mesh normally consists of several layers and hierarchies of overset grids, to resolve the motions of propellers or thrusters meanwhile capturing the ship dynamics. A typical case as demonstrated in Fig. 5 consists of a number of grid around 10.0 M. The time-step for the computation to march forward has to be sufficiently small to solve for the propeller blade rotational motion. Pressure over the ship's hull and its appendages are integrated to a force and moment matrix and feed into the 6-DoF motion equations of the vessel with respect to its centre of gravity. The solved ship motions are inherited to the overset region of the computational domain at each time step, and perform hole-cutting, and flow interpolation between reconstructed stencils. The MASS self-propulsion case in Fig. 5 utilised 600 CPUs on NSCC, and was computed for 120 h to produce a simulation of vessel motions lasts 60 s. The simulation provides a full-order prediction of the vessel's states (motions & velocities) over time when it is undertaking prescribed steering actions. System identification techniques such as the Support Vector Machine [6] and the Extended Kalman Filter [12] are intended to be applied on the full-order CFD results to derive the mathematical model of the MASS.

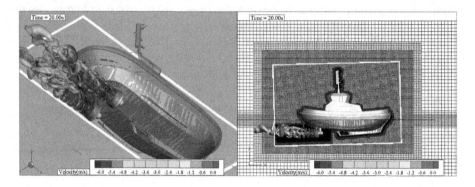

Fig. 5. Free running manoeuvring simulation of a conceptual MASS featuring thruster induced vortices and overset grid movement

The carried out computations also enable us to gain deeper understanding of the MASS' hydrodynamics under environmental disturbances. Figure 6 is one of the cases we carried out to investigate the seakeeping behaviour of our MASS design. The focus here is to evaluate the second-order mean drift force in surge

Fig. 6. Computation of TCOMS' conceptual MASS design advancing in regular waves

direction, which is also known as the wave added resistance. Both model and full scale computations are carried out in order to minimise uncertainties of scale effects. The numerical case consists 15.0M grids, and requires 600 CPUs to run for 5–7 days for each scenario.

Another aspect that is vital for the development of MASS hydrodynamic digital twin is the mathematical model of the azimuth thrusters, which is represented as torque and thrust curves under a variety of inflow conditions. Figure 7 presents the attempts we made for quantifying the thruster performance through RANS based CFD simulations. A typical CFD computation here consists of 4.0 to 5.5M mesh grids, and normally runs on 120 CPUs for approximately 24 h of wall time. More parametric studies will be carried out in near future to capture more complex flow physics involved in hull-thruster and thruster-thruster interactions. Studies on how to optimise the grid and domain discretisation while retaining the required accuracy of the solutions are ongoing to ease the computational burden as much as possible.

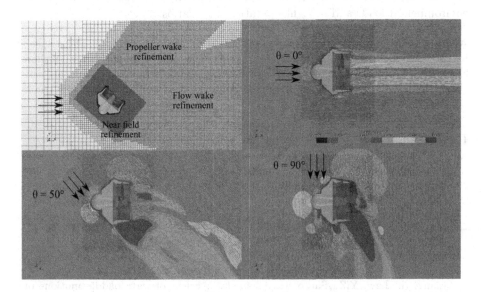

Fig. 7. Computation to evaluate the performance of TCOMS' generic design of azimuth thrusters

5   Concluding Remarks

In this paper, we have provided examples of how high-fidelity simulations of fluid-structure interactions are used to investigate the complex wave generation and interaction in the TCOMS DOB, the small-scale 'jetting effects' and the possible generation of undesirable higher-harmonic waves. The former example can be considered to be an initial effort into the creation of a digital twin of the wave basin facility, complemented by the deeper understanding local flow phenomena provided by the latter. These efforts, together with other research and development work being undertaken at TCOMS, will pave the way towards the development of a coupled numerical-physical modelling capabilities.

We have also described the digital twinning of MASS through the use of full-order CFD simulations, where the seakeeping and manoeuvring characteristics of vessel, as well as the propulsive performance of the thrusters are captured. This effort will be extended in the coming months to include parametric studies to account for interactions between each of the two thrusters, as well as between the thruster and the ship hull. Outputs from the parametric studies and the simulations of the full vessel model will subsequently be used to evolve data-driven models that will enable real-time predictions of how the MASS will behave and respond under various control inputs and environmental conditions. This is necessary for the development of autonomous navigation systems that is able to accurately steer the vessel along the planned route, under the influence of environmental loads and in tight operational scenarios.

Acknowledgements. This research is supported by A*STAR Science and Engineering Research Council with grant number 172 19 00089 under the Marine & Offshore Strategic Research Programme (M&O SRP). The computational work for this article was performed on resources of the National Supercomputing Centre, Singapore (https://www.nscc.sg).

References

1. Balay, S., et al.: PETSc Web page (2019). https://www.mcs.anl.gov/petsc
2. Ferziger, J.H., Perić, M.: Computational Methods for Fluid Dynamics. Springer, Cham (2020). https://doi.org/10.1007/978-3-319-99693-6_9
3. Hadzic, H.: Development and application of finite volume method for the computation of flows around moving bodies on unstructured, overlapping grids. Technische Universität Hamburg (2006)
4. Lee, S., Wolberg, G., Shin, S.Y.: Scattered data interpolation with multilevel B-splines. IEEE Trans. Vis. Comput. Graph. **3**(3), 228–244 (1997)
5. Liang, H., Law, Y.Z., Santo, H., Chan, E.S.: Effect of wave paddle motions on water waves. In: Proceeding of the 34th International Workshop on Water Waves and Floating Bodies, Newcastle, Australia (2019)
6. Liu, B., Jin, Y., Magee, A., Yiew, L., Zhang, S.: System identification of Abkowitz model for ship maneuvering motion based on ε-support vector regression. In: ASME: 38th International Conference on Ocean. American Society of Mechanical Engineers Digital Collection, Offshore and Arctic Engineering (2019)
7. Menter, F.R.: Two-equation eddy-viscosity turbulence models for engineering applications. AIAA J. **32**(8), 1598–1605 (1994)
8. Muzaferija, S.: Computation of free surface flows using interface-tracking and interface-capturing methods. In: Nonlinear Water-Wave Interaction, Computational Mechanics, Southampton (1998)
9. Savitzky, A., Golay, M.J.E.: Smoothing and differentiation of data by simplified least squares procedures. Anal. Chem. **36**(8), 1627–1639 (1964)

10. Shao, Y.L., Faltinsen, O.M.: A harmonic polynomial cell (HPC) method for 3D Laplace equation with application in marine hydrodynamics. J. Comput. Phys. **274**, 312–332 (2014)
11. Wu, G.X., Eatock Taylor, R.: Time stepping solutions of the two-dimensional nonlinear wave radiation problem. Ocean Eng. **22**(8), 785–798 (1995)
12. Yiew, L.J., Jin, Y., Magee, A.R.: On estimating the hydrodynamic coefficients and environmental loads for a free-running vessel in waves. In: Journal of Physics: Conference Series, vol. 1357, p. 012007. IOP Publishing (2019)

Correcting Job Walltime
in a Resource-Constrained Environment

Jessi Christa Rubio$^{(\boxtimes)}$, Aira Villapando$^{(\boxtimes)}$, Christian Matira,
and Jeffrey Aborot

Department of Science and Technology, Advanced Science and Technology Institute,
Quezon City, Philippines
{jessi,aira.villapando,christianmatira,jep}@asti.dost.gov.ph
http://asti.dost.gov.ph

Abstract. A resource-constrained HPC system such as the Computing and Archiving Research Environment (COARE) facility provides a collaborative platform for researchers to run computationally intensive experiments to address societal issues. However, users encounter job processing delays that result in low research productivity. Known causes come from the limited system capacity and the relatively long and rarely modified default walltime. In this study, we selected and characterized real HPC workloads. Then, we reviewed and applied the recommended runtime or walltime-based predictive-corrective scheduling techniques to reduce long job queues and scheduling slowdown. Using simulations to determine walltime scheduling performances on environments with limited capacity, we proved that our proposed walltime correction, especially its simple version, is enough to increase scheduling productivity. Our experiments significantly reduced the average bounded scheduling slowdown in COARE by 98.95% with a predictive-corrective approach, and 99.90% with a correction-only algorithm. Systems with large job diversity as well as those comprising of mostly short jobs significantly lowered delays and slowdown, notably with walltime correction. These simulation results strengthen our recommendation to resource-constrained system administrators to start utilizing walltime correction even without prediction to eventually increase HPC productivity.

Keywords: Resource-constrained environment · Walltime ·
Prediction · Correction · Job scheduling

1 Introduction

High-performance computing (HPC) systems comparable to the Computing and Archiving Research Environment (COARE) [1] of the Department of Science and Technology - Advanced Science and Technology Institute (DOST-ASTI) cater to

Supported by the Department of Science and Technology - Advanced Science and Technology Institute.

D. K. Panda (Ed.): SCFA 2020, LNCS 12082, pp. 118–137, 2020.
https://doi.org/10.1007/978-3-030-48842-0_8

data scientists and researchers who have growing demands for computing power. In particular, COARE HPC users work on computationally intensive research to address societal issues such as rice genome analysis for securing public health nutrition [2] and flood hazard mapping for disaster preparedness [3]. These studies are relevant and applicable to highly urbanized areas. On the path to modernizing solutions to these pressing concerns, initiatives from several research institutes in the country (in partnership with COARE) encounter hindrances in their resources. COARE and similar facilities have capacity limitations because of policy and budgetary constraints in operational and capital expenditures. Especially for government research institutes, it may take a while to enact new policy changes [4,5] and to add more compute and storage servers that must undergo a notoriously long procurement process [6]. Thus, a shared environment among researchers where they can collaborate and concurrently calculate solutions to complex computing tasks is essential. Practicing resource management or job scheduling enables this sharing. Improving job scheduling performance then becomes crucial to optimizing the usage of resource-constrained HPC systems.

Such systems practice default job scheduling configuration with the *walltime request* (WTR) set to the maximum. Depending on the demand for longer simulation, COARE sets a default WTR to 7 or 14 days for all jobs. System administrators approximated this WTR setting based on the runtimes of the first few jobs that had been submitted to the facility when its operations began. The scheduler reads this walltime or *kill time* as the hard limit to process a job to give way for other jobs to run. However, not all jobs take as long as the estimated walltime to finish; most jobs need just under a day to complete. Furthermore, COARE users rarely adjust their WTRs (see Sect. 3.1) and instead use the default settings. This situation introduces inaccurate scheduling, which hampers processing more jobs. Moreover, setting the walltime to the maximum disables the backfilling of small and lower priority jobs [7]. From our analysis of jobs submitted to COARE (detailed in Sect. 2), most of these encounter long job queues to give way to higher priority ones that have huge computational resource requirements to finish. This processing delay has been one of the most pressing critical complaints of the COARE HPC users.

For years, several researchers continue to analyze and perform thorough development of walltime-based scheduling to improve scheduling accuracy [8–10]. In this work, we analyzed how COARE and other resource-constrained HPC systems (defined in Sect. 3) can take advantage of existing predictive-corrective WTR-based scheduling algorithms (expounded in Sect. 4). Specifically, we contribute the following:

- walltime corrective algorithms *even without prediction* can reduce scheduling slowdown and eventually eliminate unwanted job delays, and
- a *simple* version of walltime correction, a more practical approach than existing corrective algorithms that systems like COARE could immediately utilize.

We additionally developed a regression-based walltime prediction that considers job size diversity and accounts more features not limited to the recommended

CPU and walltime [11] to ensure finer predictions. After performing scheduling simulations (Sect. 5) on identified real HPC workloads, our results (Sect. 6) proved a significant increase in scheduling productivity. We conducted this study to gain useful insights to revise current HPC operations policies not only for COARE but to guide similar resource-constrained environments as well.

2   Productivity in Resource-Constrained HPC Systems

2.1   Job Delays

Of the total responses on DOST-ASTI COARE's client satisfaction survey, 30.5% have reservations on the performance and reliability of the service with the current system. Not only is there a high demand for faster and larger computational power, but there were also helpful comments on long job queues. In particular, an end-user raised his concern about experiencing a one-week waiting time for one of his jobs. A week's time is the default walltime in COARE, which primarily contributed to the long waiting time. About 99.5% of the total jobs from COARE have waiting times of less than 3 days. These 198,386 jobs, however, should not discount the 142 jobs that queued for more than 7 days, as depicted in Table 1. These queued jobs generally had large CPU and memory requirements that could not necessarily fit available nodes. If these large jobs have short run times, more than 7 days of waiting could really be frustrating especially if the user's experiment is highly relevant in creating social impact.

Table 1. Distribution of jobs in COARE grouped according to their waiting time.

Waiting time (days)	No. of jobs
<3	198,386
[3, 7)	526
[7, 14)	115
≥14	27

Upgrading the facility's computational capacity faces challenges that require careful planning to meet growing demands and adhere to existing policies. Because of operational and capital cost restrictions for each fiscal year, the length of time to acquire such equipment could render longer productivity delays or, worse, obsolete hardware by the time it operates at the production level. Capacity management, though recommended [6], is still an ongoing process and is yet to be established in COARE. Given these limitations, it is imperative to find ways to maximize usage with existing resources such as shortening job queues. Reducing job delays requires implementing an accurate walltime scheduling.

2.2   Walltime Accuracy Effect on Productivity

Since walltime is user-specified, walltime accuracy may depend on its closeness to the actual runtime in terms of underestimates or overestimates. A job with *underestimated* runtime gets paused or killed if the WTR is less than its actual duration. Meanwhile, *overestimation* hinders the scheduler to correctly organize jobs because the compute nodes are already reserved for other jobs. This situation is particularly evident when most or all WTRs are set to the maximum default timelimit [7], which resembles the case in COARE. Alike resource-constrained systems suffer from inaccurate scheduling that leads to long queues. Because of the limited hardware capacity and an increase in the number of users, more jobs need to be processed in the same period, subsequently resulting in even longer queues. These job delays imply an irony of performing high-speed calculations, which defeats productivity. The length of a job correlates to the user acceptance of the waiting time [12]. Hence, if most jobs have small resource requirements and shorter runtimes get stuck in a long queue, their waiting time consequently increases. This scenario then becomes unacceptable.

3   Understanding Real HPC Workloads

3.1   Walltime Charactertics

If we look closely, Fig. 1 shows that COARE is mostly comprised of fixed walltime requests at either 7 or 14 days, which demonstrate overestimates with the maximum timelimit. Sizeable wide gaps between the actual runtime and the WTR are observable. These differences cause scheduling walltime inaccuracies. Though real and large computer systems from the Parallel Workloads Archive [13] may not fully represent resource-constrained facilities, we used several of these workloads in comparison to COARE's that depict real-world scenarios for reproducibility. Alternatively, we could use the simulated results from these workloads to find out if correction-only WTR scheduling is sufficient and applicable for large HPC systems. We selected workloads from the archive that are similar to COARE, which comprise jobs with diverse or *heterogeneous* geometries [14]. This heterogeneity is currently an architectural trend in HPC systems [15].

A comparable workload is from the University of Luxembourg Gaia Cluster [16], which also portrays differences between runtime and WTR but at minimal distinction. MetaCentrum2 [17] has larger WTR and runtime gaps similar to COARE's but more accurate WTRs at the latter part. The CEA Curie system [18] primarily consists of jobs having runtime and WTR difference slightly distinguishable and within a day's length. To extend our analysis to other possible HPC setups beyond the small heterogeneous systems, we consider the large Curie workload and the homogeneous HPC2N Seth workload [19]. Further, with the Gaia workload primarily composed of specialized biological and engineering computing experiments and the homogeneous Seth workload, these systems may represent resource-constrained environments dedicated to specific scientific

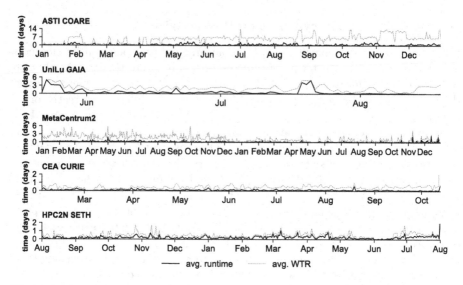

Fig. 1. Daily average job walltime requests and daily average job runtimes in various real HPC systems.

applications. Less variation in the job sizes in a homogeneous workload could mean similar experiments. As observed in Fig. 1, the Seth workload depicts an ideal case of walltime estimates that are comparable to job duration.

3.2 Job Diversity and Walltime Scheduling

Job geometry or size refers to a combination of compute and walltime resources [14]. Jobs with small geometry may consist of a few compute requirements and short walltime while large ones may be composed of hundreds of CPUs and may span for days. In Fig. 2, we characterized the jobs of each selected HPC workload to give context on their job geometry distribution and to learn how this variation in job sizes influences scheduling performance. We applied hexbin plotting of the workloads, where each bin constitutes the number of counts for each number of CPU and runtime combination as represented in the color bar for guidance. These plots require logarithmic scaling of the bins to easily differentiate the small jobs from the large ones. To elucidate further, small jobs take the bottom left corner of the plot while longer jobs occupy the right side. This representation allowed us to understand the implications of workload heterogeneity among HPC clusters with respect to scheduling policies presented in Table 2.

The COARE workload (Fig. 2a), as well as the MetaCentrum2 (Fig. 2c), consists of predominantly small jobs and notably long jobs with small CPU requirements and long runtime. With a relatively wide distribution of large or long jobs, we can say that the COARE workload is highly heterogeneous or diverse. Also heterogeneous, the Gaia workload (Fig. 2b) has a good concentration of jobs at

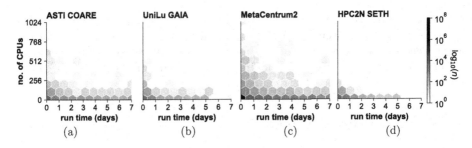

Fig. 2. Job size distribution of HPC workloads from (a) ASTI COARE, (b) UniLu Gaia, (c) MetaCentrum2 and (d) HPC2N Seth where the color bar represents a scaled count n of each hexbin, given by $\log_{10}(n)$.

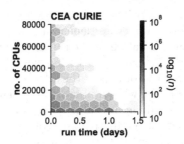

Fig. 3. Job size distribution of workload from CEA CURIE.

Table 2. Scheduling scenarios of predictive and corrective policies.

WTR policy	Prediction	Correction
user-estimate	none	user-estimates
EASY++	AVE_2	simple
		power
regression	$AdaBoost$	simple
		power
simple	none	simple
power	none	power

the bottom and the left corner depicting small jobs mainly with a dispersed set of long jobs. Similar to Gaia, the homogeneous Seth (Fig. 2d) has mostly short jobs concentrated at the bottom left corner. On one hand, the expansive Curie workload may have short jobs with less than a day's duration but these jobs have huge CPU requirements (Fig. 3). Given these workloads, we also must note that results may vary from one workload to another [20].

Heterogeneity in a workload may decrease the job waiting time predictability: the more diverse the job geometries, the harder it is to determine when jobs would finish [14]. In an environment with high job diversity such as those in resource-constrained systems, there must be a way to refine scheduling requirements such as having accurate WTRs. To reduce long queues, accurate walltime will enable the scheduler to precisely assign jobs to allocated nodes [21]. Thus for heterogeneous workloads, developing accurate walltime prediction becomes relevant in the scheduling performance.

4   Walltime-Based Scheduling

4.1   Walltime Prediction and Correction

The goal of WTR-based prediction is to generate walltime values close to the actual duration for efficient scheduling. *Prediction* techniques along with *correction* and *backfilling* algorithms form a *heuristic triple* in walltime-based scheduling [11]. Scheduling performance varies depending on the combination of algorithms in the triple. As an illustration, if the runtime should reach the predicted walltime and the job is not yet done, correcting the kill time will prevent premature job termination. Instead of letting the scheduler kill jobs based on user-estimates, corrective techniques will automatically extend the walltime of jobs either incrementally or by doubling its value before the kill time.

We derived combinations of predictive and corrective algorithms and compared these to a user-estimate walltime request-based scheduling (see Table 2 for a summary of scheduling scenarios). We define *user-estimates* as user-specified approximates of their jobs' runtime. The existing practice in HPCs similar to COARE is to set user-estimate walltime request as the kill time.

The *user-estimate* scheduling has no predictive algorithm, but it allows the user to indicate the job walltime. In the case of COARE, user-estimates are generally the default WTR values. This prevents the continuation of jobs with duration more than the walltime. If set too high relative to the mean duration of all jobs, the scheduler will fail to accurately estimate the length of jobs. This will cause jobs to pile up leading to a long queue. To counter this inefficiency, a walltime-based predictive approach empowers the scheduler to have better foresight of each job's probable duration and thus precisely assigns jobs to appropriate resources. Prediction comes best with correction when avoiding underestimated walltime.

In the third part of the triple, the scheduler backfills queued jobs to available nodes. An efficient strategy is to backfill the shortest job first as it is with the EASY++-SJBF [7]. Along with backfilling, the EASY++-SJBF implements averaging the runtime of the previous two jobs of the same user to predict the walltime and automatically increases the time limit to correct underestimates. Because backfilling is already in effect in the COARE's scheduler, we focused on analyzing the triple's prediction and correction parts (as in Table 2) and set the backfilling configuration as fixed. We did this to differentiate and isolate the scheduling improvements brought by walltime prediction and correction.

4.2   User-Based Prediction

Another prediction method uses *soft* walltime estimates by taking as a factor the most accurate walltime with respect to the previous job duration of the same user [9]. If the posted walltime becomes underpredicted, the soft method then kills the job once its runtime reaches the user estimate. Setting the predictor to use the past 2 jobs as a reference would suffice [7] compared to considering all past jobs' duration.

While both EASY++ and soft techniques employ prediction, the accuracy of the prediction becomes limited due to its user-based only characteristics. These methods are dependent on the historical job duration of the same user. Predicting the walltime on the assumption that users consecutively run the same experiment fails to recognize that these jobs may have different lengths. Illustratively, if the user sequentially runs a 2-h job and another at 16 h, how are we certain that the next job is within their 9-h average? Correction (detailed in Sect. 4.4) becomes helpful at this point as it extends the walltime should there be an underestimation. This leads us to another question, how often does this case of the same user with different jobs occur?

Upon inspecting the distribution of runtime per user in COARE, numerous users have jobs of different lengths. Dissecting this distribution aids in analyzing how runtime varies for every user.

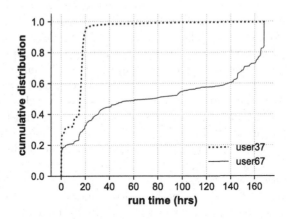

Fig. 4. Runtime distribution of user37 and user67 in COARE.

Looking closely at the job runtimes of user67 in Fig. 4, around 80% of its jobs were largely varying from 15 to 165 h. On the contrary, 65% of jobs submitted by user37 had runtimes ranging at a narrow 15 to 25 h. From these observations, we deduced that the prediction in EASY++ will be ineffective in user67 but will yield more accurate WTR in user37. We cannot say the EASY++ prediction would work properly if the user67 and the like scenario happens frequently. For this study, we are curious on how effective predictive algorithms are in the scheduling process because if correction would always take place then this would be enough and we no longer need to implement prediction.

4.3   User and Job-Based Prediction

The same user's jobs that have similar characteristics may also have comparable runtime though not necessarily submitted consecutively. To incorporate both user and job-based prediction, an existing scheduling algorithm alerts users of potential underestimates wherein the jobs are patterned on the runtime behavior of other jobs from the same scientific application [10]. The premise of this algorithm approximates the duration of jobs meant for solving a particular type of differential equation problem the same runtime as future jobs of similar nature. But this algorithm focuses on walltime underestimates only and would require a large database of experiments and their runtime behavior that may result in inefficient scheduling. Further, scientific applications vary from one computer system to another. Other resource-constrained environments collaborating with COARE either have specific patterns of experimental calculations or cater to experiments that are as diverse as research from different scientific fields [2]. A numerical modeling type of problem has a myriad of resource requirements and the extent of this variation must be carefully considered when adopting this job-based prediction to actual HPC systems.

Narrowing the job-based prediction to available standard workload logs [13] instead of depending on the jobs' scientific application, a *regression* model can consider CPU resource and walltime requests of each job. This method is distinctly relevant for those with large geometries as predicting this type of job properly will lead to better scheduling performance [11]. Because most schedulers rely on the CPU requirement, gauging other job features, such as burst buffers when it comes to I/O intensive processing, can lead to improved performance [22]. With the available parameters from the workload logs in mind, we disregarded burst buffer then we accounted for other features such as memory size. As recommended [11], we developed a regression-based prediction of runtime estimates suited for COARE with more features considered other than CPU and WTR to ensure finer prediction accuracy.

We implemented our version of this prediction using the established AdaBoost algorithm [23] in conjunction with decision trees to extract potential runtime in a *regression* manner (see Algorithm 1). Instead of utilizing both squared and linear error functions as suggested [11], we applied the closely comparable AdaBoost, a commonly implemented and relatively accurate regression model for prediction [24]. For every learning iteration m, the model equally weighs WTR predictions made by fitting the decision tree regressor, $y_m(x)$, regardless of accuracy to minimize the linear error function

$$J_m = \sum_{i=1}^{N} w_i^{(m)} I[y_i(x_n) \neq h_i(x_m)], \tag{1}$$

where h is an output hypothesis. AdaBoost works by tweaking these weights resulting from the first learner depending on the error of prediction. The larger

---

Algorithm 1. *regression*-based WTR policy using AdaBoost

Input: dataset of size n with feature space X_n and runtime Y_n, weak learner *decision tree*

Output: regression model $F(x)$

1: Initialize the data weights w_n.
2: **for** $m = 1$ to M **do**
3:    fit decision tree regressor $y_m(x)$ by minimizing weighted error function J_m
4:    compute for the weighted training error ϵ_m
5:    evaluate coefficient $\alpha_m = \log(\frac{1-\epsilon_m}{\epsilon_m})$
6:    update data weights $w_n^{(m+1)}$
7: **end for**
8: predict using the final model $F(x) = \text{sign}(\sum_{m=1}^{M} \alpha_m y_m(x))$

---

the prediction error ϵ_m, the smaller and more negative the weight w_n becomes. The predicted WTR is the weighted median prediction by the learners. In this writing, we considered working on historical data from X_n features comprising *user*, *job runtime*, and *requested CPU* and *memory* resources. In the instance that a job continues to run within 60 s of the estimated WTR, the scheduling invokes a corrective algorithm. A potential downfall of this regression technique lies in the large historical data that the prediction has to always check which could lead to an even greater slowdown.

If the same user adjusted the compute requirements of the same experiment say requested for 60 CPUs instead, then the length of the new job's duration will most probably be different. The regression approach assumes that the same user can run different experiments at various points in time, contrary to EASY++. If the same user has another experiment with the same compute requirements, specifically numerical modeling this time compared to last time's statistical analysis, and the duration becomes 10 h, then prediction in the regression should still be effective because duration is one of the assumed features and will correctly classify the change as an entirely different experiment.

4.4 Correction

As indicated in Table 2, the predictive-corrective *EASY++* [7] engages a technique to predict the runtime and then increments the walltime before the premature termination of jobs with underestimated walltime. Correction can be in the form of user-estimates or doubling WTRs [11]. Another form is the *power* function $15 \times 2^{i-2}$, where $i = 2, \ldots, n$ minutes, as exercised in EASY++ and proven to deliver more accurate WTRs than the other correction methods. Aside from the power correction, we considered a simpler approach to correct the underestimated walltime. We invoked our version of an incremental walltime correction called *simple* as soon as the current runtime of a job reaches 60 s before the set walltime (see Algorithm 2).

The simple corrective method basically checks if a job is still running within a minute of its set time limit. If it is, the scheduler will automatically extend the

---

Algorithm 2. *simple* walltime correction

Input: job object instance *job*, user-estimate walltime WTR, job start time *s*, current
    running time *t*

Output: updated walltime WTR

 1: Query current running job by user *job*.user_id.
 2: **while** *job*.user_id is RUNNING **do**
 3:   **if** WTR $-\, t < 60$ **then**
 4:     **if** $0 \leq t - s \leq 604800$ **then**
 5:       WTR $=$ WTR $+\, 3600$
 6:     **end if**
 7:   **end if**
 8: **end while**

---

walltime limit to 1 h. It continues to check and update the time limit until the
job completes or the hard time limit of 7 days is reached, whichever comes first.

Figure 5 details a comparison of the two corrective techniques and how fast
their correction would reach a job's actual duration. Correction stops as soon as
the corrected walltime is greater than or equal to the runtime. At iteration 0,
WTRs of jobs are arbitrarily initialized to 2 h and 6 h. This headstart represents
the set walltime prediction before correction takes place. For an 8-h job, a 6-h
headstart is a closer prediction than 2 h. If prediction is more accurate, then
the simple method will approach the runtime sooner and will produce accurate
walltime scheduling. Conversely, if prediction is bad, the power method converges
faster with the actual duration.

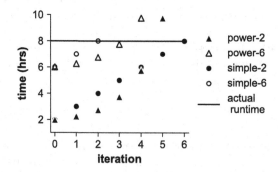

Fig. 5. Walltime iteration comparison of the two correction methods with respect to
actual runtimes arbitrarily given 2-h (in black) and 6-h (in white) headstart.

To determine how correction-only algorithms perform compared to
predictive-corrective ones, we implemented the proposed simple and the power
correction WTR policies and assumed a default prediction of 10 min. Setting
prediction to this value invokes underestimation that should trigger correction.
Based on the runtime distribution of our identified workloads (see Fig. 6 and

Sect. 3.1 for more information), most jobs are approximately less than 1 h. Thus, to ensure underprediction takes place, we kept the default to 10 min instead of 1 h or 10 h or more.

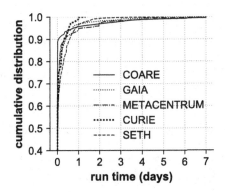

Fig. 6. Cumulative distribution of jobs with respect to runtime of various real HPC workloads.

Walltime underestimation from coarse-grained user-estimates is seen as the primary source of scheduling inaccuracies [9–11,25]. Predicting walltime is likewise prone to error that correction could address. This strategy avoids lost scheduling opportunities in overestimation and reduces the gap between the user-estimates and the actual runtime. If the correction part is always taking place, then we can disregard prediction and implement correction-only in the scheduling. Moreover, if correction even without prediction improves scheduling performance in resource-constrained facilities, then we can therefore solidify our recommendation to adopt this policy to other similar HPC environments.

5 Experimental Setup

5.1 Workload Preparation

To demonstrate our idea, we performed simulations on the WTR policies (Table 2) using several real HPC workloads. If we repeat the same test scenario, simulation results will not converge [20]. Hence, to conduct reliable experimentation, we tested the reproducibility of our assumptions by comparing job traces from DOST-ASTI COARE to other computer systems from the Parallel Workloads Archive [13]. Specifically, we implemented our theories by simulating workloads from the UniLu Gaia (2014-2 logs [16]) and MetaCentrum2 (2013-3 logs [17]). We sampled the MetaCentrum2 workload to one month period of the most recent jobs to simplify our simulations. These workloads are from heterogeneous systems similar to COARE's. We additionally examined the workload from the CEA Curie (2011-2.1 cleaned logs [18]), likewise heterogeneous, which comprises of more than 93,000 CPUs that may not accurately represent a resource-constrained environment. We regard the Curie system in our experiments since it utilizes the same scheduler as COARE's called Slurm (to be discussed in Sect. 4.2). Including this workload in our experiments will help us understand how large HPC systems influence predictive-corrective walltime scheduling performance. Further, we considered the HPC2N Seth (using the 2002-2.2 clean version [19]) to include homogeneous systems, expanding our simulations to other probable HPC setup in terms of job size distribution. Table 3 illustrates selected features of each computer system.

Table 3. Generic composition of real HPC workloads used in the experiments.

	DOST-ASTI COARE	UniLu Gaia	MetaCentrum2	CEA Curie	HPC2N Seth
No. of jobs (cleaned)	199, 054	51, 834	197, 368	11, 268	45, 333
No. of nodes	48	151	495	5, 544	240
No. of CPUs	2, 304	2, 004	8, 412	93, 312	240
Period (month)	12	3	1	1	12

There were specific workload anomalies that must be filtered [8] depending on the system. For instance, the Curie workload log portion considered contains jobs submitted only after February 2012. This takes into account the changes made in the infrastructure design since 2011. In HPC2N Seth, we removed flurry of very high activity by a single user, which constitutes more than 55% of the whole log. Finally, we disregarded all jobs that ran for more than 7 days across all HPC systems. These filters were generally applied to remove occurrences of flurries that could introduce unwanted biases.

In aggregating our simulation results, we removed the first 1% of the simulated jobs as prescribed [7]. This would help reduce the warm-up effects brought about by the learning period at the start of the prediction algorithms.

As of this writing, the COARE workload log in SWF format as prescribed [20] as well as other relevant scripts used in this work are available online [26].

5.2   Scheduling Simulator

The Slurm Workload Manager (Slurm) [27] is a widely adopted open-source workload manager for various HPC environments. This tool facilitates the concurrent running of multiple experiments or jobs through a scheduling algorithm to assign jobs to server nodes. Because COARE uses Slurm as its scheduler, we performed our experiments using a Slurm simulator [28].

We adjusted the Slurm simulator source code to carry out either simple or power correction algorithms, as required (see Table 2). Likewise, we modified the Slurm configuration scripts to suit system setup such as nodes, processors and memory specifications for each workload [1, 16–19]. We selected appropriate data fields from the SWF that are in congruence with the Slurm simulator and then converted it into CSV format. A pre-processing tool from the Slurm simulator package would read the CSV file and then translate it into a binary equivalent that the simulator will process.

The SWF, in an attempt to create a generalized workload format, considers only bare minimum parameters. This discrepancy means that the Slurm simulator would require parameters, particularly the number of nodes (n-nodes) and the number of tasks (n-tasks), that are not explicitly specified in workloads in SWF. Closely related to these data fields, the SWF consists of number of CPUs per job only and each workload generalizes the total system node count information instead of node count per job. To supply the simulator with these missing SWF parameters, we modeled a decision tree regressor (apart from the one discussed in Sect. 4.3) according to COARE users' behavior and fitted it to relevant parameters in other workloads.

The decision tree regressor, which is a machine learning model, predicts values based on a logic-based tree structure [29], and is inherently non-parametric. This means prediction would still be reliable even if the distribution is not normal. Compared to a single source of learning input with the traditional linear regression, we utilized the decision tree logic to consider several features of the workload format compatible with the simulator. Because the raw COARE workload log follows through Slurm accounting, it provides data fields congruent to what the Slurm simulator requires. In this case, our input training data were from the COARE workload, where we used the *number of CPUs*, *required memory*, *WTR*, and *runtime* as predictor variables. The regressor would learn from the trend of the input training workload parameters based on the decision tree logic to produce predictions of n-nodes and n-tasks.

Because COARE has a maximum of 48 CPUs per node, systems of less capacity could still encounter inaccurate regressor predictions should the requested number of nodes exceed the system's limit. Based on the 48 CPU per node in COARE, the regressor model would return 2 nodes only for a 96 CPU request which a 36 CPU per node system would insufficiently service 72 CPUs at most. To address this error, we divided the 96 CPUs by the system's CPU per node limit and used its ceiling result of 3 nodes instead.

Before running a simulation, we recompiled the simulator to read changes in the source code, and then repopulated the database with the new configuration. Upon generating a job trace file, we can then run an experiment to simulate the scheduling process. Also, simulation time lags with respect to increasing node count [28]. Therefore, we limited our analysis to shorter time ranges for some workloads (as in Sect. 5.1).

5.3   Performance Metric

We utilized the average wait time metric to evaluate the effectiveness of each scheduling policy, as is recommended to have better convergence [20]. The wait time ω is equivalent to the absolute difference between the submit time (T_{submit}) of a job to the time it starts running (T_{start}) or $|T_{\text{submit}} - T_{\text{start}}|$. Note that this wait time is exclusive of the runtime and returns results in seconds. To better realize the delay effect on productivity, instead of seconds, we converted the results into minutes in our analysis. Greater ω value means more job processing delays, which consequently entails lowered user and system productivity.

To validate our results further, we used the average bounded slowdown ($avgBSLD$) of the scheduler as practiced [7, 11, 20]. We defined this performance metric as

$$avgBSLD = \frac{1}{n} \sum \max \left(\frac{\omega + R}{\max(R, \tau)}, 1 \right),$$ (2)

where R is the actual runtime, and τ is a threshold value, set to 10 s as generally practiced. The max function guarantees that each job's $BSLD$ should be greater than or equal to 1 to ensure boundedness in the results. The $avgBSLD$ would then result to a factor such that the greater its value, scheduling slows down even more and likewise impedes overall HPC productivity.

6   Simulation Results Analysis

In this section, we consolidated the results of our simulations and analyzed the WTR policies' impact on resource-constrained HPC systems. Again, in this paper, our goal is to evaluate the effectiveness of implementing predictive-corrective scheduling to resource-constrained systems like COARE. We used this evaluation to support our proposal that correction can independently reduce job processing delays in terms of wait time and slowdown metrics. Because of the accurate WTRs in Gaia, Seth, MetaCentrum2 and Curie, using the user-estimate as the baseline for the other policies would lead to incomparable improvement results. Instead, we compared these WTR policies from one another in all workloads.

6.1   Wait Time Performance

Upon comparing workloads from one another (Table 4), we can immediately observe that the wait time performances among scheduling policies are not discernible enough to differentiate any improvement in COARE. We associate this discrepancy from getting the mean of jobs which are mostly with less than 3 days wait time (in Table 1). To resolve this inconsistency, we considered looking into the $avgBSLD$ metric (to be discussed in Sect. 6.2).

Again, the sampled MetaCentrum2 workload used in the simulation (Sect. 5.1) has more accurate user-estimates than COARE. Thus the improvement in the other policies are at a minimum. All predictive-corrective policies have less than 30 min of ω. A 30-min wait time is generally not deterrent to user productivity compared to COARE's waiting time range as depicted in Table 1. The EASY++-simple ω of around 21 min considerably reduced waiting time at most 7 min in comparison to the other WTR policies.

Also, keep in mind that Gaia and Seth workloads have similar job diversity (Fig. 2) as well as closer WTRs to the actual duration compared to COARE (Fig. 1). The predictive-corrective ω performance of the Gaia workload exhibited

Table 4. Average wait time (in minutes) among workloads for each WTR policy.

	DOST-ASTI COARE	UniLu Gaia	MetaCentrum2	CEA Curie	HPC2N Seth
user-estimate	4.89	260.96	28.21	313.94	93.38
EASY++ (power)	5.01	289.54	28.09	234.94	111.13
EASY++ (simple)	4.88	185.93	21.50	237.62	108.66
regression (power)	4.95	247.22	25.68	183.37	53.09
regression (simple)	5.16	243.91	25.75	171.31	52.61
power	4.85	1,148.76	28.05	148.20	70.00
simple	4.90	1,137.67	26.93	151.41	59.63

interesting results where the EASY++ prediction produced a closer headstart and elicited speedier approach to the actual duration with simple and lagged with power. Regression is at a point where its prediction is not as accurate as EASY++ but close enough to the actual runtime compared to those of the plain corrective methods. The extremely negative simple and power correction results in this workload showed the necessity for a more accurate walltime prediction. We can observe the same pattern in the Seth's wait time results but the EASY++ yielded inaccurate predictions compared to regression and even in correction. The EASY++ predictions cannot go below where a correction-only algorithm started and thus resulted in walltime overestimation. Even if the jobs are mostly short in these workloads, regression works best when the same user runs consecutive jobs of different sizes. For resource-constrained systems with job geometry distribution as Gaia and Seth, the simple correction along with an appropriate prediction method can promise favorable results.

Meanwhile, the large Curie workload generated a sizeable wait time reduction for all policies. Again, regression produced more accurate predictions than EASY++ because of the high variation among job sizes in the workload. Simple and power correction methods in Curie were almost the same. Across all HPC clusters in our experiments, the correction-only method in a large system primarily composed of short jobs though big ones garnered the most distinguishable improvement with a notable 160 min or 2.7 h reduced waiting time compared to the user-estimate in the Curie workload.

6.2   Scheduling Slowdown

The wait time experiments generated varying outcomes across HPC systems. At this point, the wait time metric is still insufficient to discern the differences from one policy to another, particularly for COARE-like systems. Hence, we derived the *avgBSLD*. Table 5 showcases the performance of predictive-corrective algorithms across workloads and at a glance, simple and power corrective algorithms produced the same outputs.

All workloads suffer heavy slowdown with walltime set to user-estimate compared to predictive-corrective algorithms. Scheduling slowdown in COARE is gravely around 29,447 *avgBSLD*. The implemented predictive-corrective policies consistently eliminated this severe scheduling slowdown in COARE by 98.95%, and by 99.90% with a correction-only approach.

The heterogeneous workloads from COARE, Gaia and Curie measurably improved with predictive-corrective scheduling. These workloads performed noteworthy slowdown reduction with EASY++ and regression compared to user-estimates. Between prediction algorithms, these HPC systems obtained an increase in slowdown with regression compared to EASY++. Because of the large number of jobs and the job size diversity in these workloads, prediction may take much time and thereby contribute to a slowdown of less than 567 in regression. Correction-only policy remarkably removed scheduling slowdown on these workloads. In large HPC systems like Curie, we recommend using a corrective-only scheduling as this yielded more beneficial results than those with prediction.

Wait time and slowdown results from the regression and corrective walltime policies both agreed in Gaia. We can observe the same pattern in Seth. Though EASY++ contributed the largest $avgBSLD$, we note that the user-estimate policy in the Seth workload also has accurate WTRs. A 650 slowdown factor is better than COARE's extreme 29,447. For systems like Gaia and Seth that are focused on specific scientific applications and composed of mostly short jobs, applying correction techniques along with an appropriate prediction strategy could greatly reduce scheduling slowdown and job processing delays.

The sampled portion of the heterogeneous MetaCentrum2 (described in Sect. 5.1) had accurate user-estimates that are as comparable to those of Seth and Gaia (refer to Fig. 1). Slowdown results in the user-estimate and predictive-corrective approaches for MetaCentrum2 were almost the same. Correction outperformed the other slowdown results from more than 739 to an improved 6 $avgBSLD$. Particularly for resource-constrained systems with large job diversity, a correction-only walltime scheduling consistently guarantees reduced performance slowdown.

Table 5. Average bounded slowdown among workloads for each WTR policy.

	DOST-ASTI COARE	UniLu Gaia	MetaCentrum2	CEA Curie	HPC2N Seth
user-estimate	29,447	1,182	806	958	637
EASY++ (power)	160	53	813	53	655
EASY++ (simple)	160	53	822	53	655
regression (power)	259	412	739	567	2
regression (simple)	259	412	739	567	2
power	30	5	6	19	16
simple	30	5	6	19	16

6.3   Results Synthesis

Understanding the characteristics of a resource-constrained system should lead to effective implementation of walltime-based scheduling. While job dependencies [9] and interarrival times [30] may have an effect on WTR accuracy, we leave this for future work. Instead in this study, we focus on analyzing the workloads along with the wait time and slowdown metrics to shed light on which WTR policy works best. Performing any predictive-corrective technique could immensely reduce delays from using user-estimates only. Resource-constrained environments similar to COARE, especially those with highly varying job size distribution, should start practicing walltime correction in their scheduling. The same goes for workloads consisting of mostly short jobs that could be catering to specific research applications. Adding prediction in these types of systems would slightly reduce scheduling slowdown up to 822 across all workloads. Thus, we suggest that walltime correction without prediction, particularly our simple version, is enough and more practical to implement in the production level.

7   Conclusion

Challenges in resource-constrained HPC systems such as COARE could be initially addressed with proper implementation of appropriate walltime prediction-correction scheduling. In this study, scrutinizing workload characteristics is essential to discern system-appropriate walltime policies. Systems with large job size diversity such as COARE produced desirable scheduling slowdown reduction with predictive-corrective algorithms and remarkably in our proposed simple corrective-only approach. We can now apply a walltime corrective-only scheduling policy in the upcoming production release of COARE's new HPC cluster. Resource-constrained environments similar to COARE can correspondingly follow through the evaluation process in this paper to fit their workload conditions and more importantly practice walltime correction even without prediction.

Acknowledgments. We thank the Department of Science and Technology - Advanced Science and Technology Institute (DOST-ASTI) for supporting us in conducting this research to improve COARE's HPC facility and user experience. We would also like to thank Arvin Lamando and most especially Jay Samuel Combinido for their invaluable contributions during the first stages of this research. Additionally, we acknowledge real HPC workload contributors from the Parallel Workloads Archive namely: Joseph Emeras for Gaia and Curie, Dalibor Klusáček for MetaCentrum2, and Ake Sandgren for Seth.

References

1. DOST-ASTI: Computing and Archiving Research Environment (COARE) (2019). https://asti.dost.gov.ph/projects/coare
2. COARE stakeholders, collaborations, and partnerships. https://asti.dost.gov.ph/coare/wiki/Main/other-info/stakeholders/
3. DOST-ASTI: DATOS remote sensing and data science help desk. https://asti.dost.gov.ph/projects/datos/
4. Morton, A.L.: Assessing policy implementation success: observations from the Philippines. World Dev. **24**(9), 1441–1451 (1996)

5. Quah, J.S.: Public bureaucracy and policy implementation in Asia: an introduction. Southeast Asian J. Soc. Sci. **15**(2), vii–xvi (1987)
6. Navarro, A., Tanghal, J.: The promises and pains in procurement reforms in the Philippines (2017). https://pidswebs.pids.gov.ph/CDN/PUBLICATIONS/pidsdps1716.pdf
7. Tsafrir, D., Etsion, Y., Feitelson, D.G.: Backfilling using system-generated predictions rather than user runtime estimates. IEEE Trans. Parallel Distrib. Syst. **18**(6), 789–803 (2007)
8. Feitelson, D.G., Tsafrir, D., Krakov, D.: Experience with using the parallel workloads archive. J. Parallel Distrib. Comput. **74**(10), 2967–2982 (2014)
9. Klusáček, D., Chlumský, V.: Evaluating the impact of soft walltimes on job scheduling performance. In: Klusáček, D., Cirne, W., Desai, N. (eds.) JSSPP 2018. LNCS, vol. 11332, pp. 15–38. Springer, Cham (2018). https://doi.org/10.1007/978-3-030-10632-4_2
10. Guo, J., Nomura, A., Barton, R., Zhang, H., Matsuoka, S.: Machine learning predictions for underestimation of job runtime on HPC system. In: Yokota, R., Wu, W. (eds.) SCFA 2018. LNCS, vol. 10776, pp. 179–198. Springer, Cham (2018). https://doi.org/10.1007/978-3-319-69953-0_11
11. Gaussier, E., Glesser, D., Reis, V., Trystram, D.: Improving backfilling by using machine learning to predict running times. In: Proceedings of the International Conference for High Performance Computing, Networking, Storage and Analysis, p. 64. ACM (2015)
12. Schlagkamp, S., Renker, J.: Acceptance of waiting times in high performance computing. In: Stephanidis, C. (ed.) HCI 2015. CCIS, vol. 529, pp. 709–714. Springer, Cham (2015). https://doi.org/10.1007/978-3-319-21383-5_120
13. Feitelson, D.G.: Parallel workloads archive. https://www.cse.huji.ac.il/labs/parallel/workload
14. Rodrigo, G.P., Östberg, P.O., Elmroth, E., Antypas, K., Gerber, R., Ramakrishnan, L.: Towards understanding HPC users and systems: a NERSC case study. J. Parallel Distrib. Comput. **111**, 206–221 (2018)
15. Flórez, E., Barrios, C.J., Pecero, J.E.: Methods for job scheduling on computational grids: review and comparison. In: Osthoff, C., Navaux, P.O.A., Barrios Hernandez, C.J., Silva Dias, P.L. (eds.) CARLA 2015. CCIS, vol. 565, pp. 19–33. Springer, Cham (2015). https://doi.org/10.1007/978-3-319-26928-3_2
16. Emeras, J.: The University of Luxembourg Gaia cluster log. https://www.cse.huji.ac.il/labs/parallel/workload/l_unilu_gaia/index.html
17. Klusáček, D., Tóth, Š., Podolníková, G.: Real-life experience with major reconfiguration of job scheduling system. In: Desai, N., Cirne, W. (eds.) JSSPP 2015-2016. LNCS, vol. 10353, pp. 83–101. Springer, Cham (2017). https://doi.org/10.1007/978-3-319-61756-5_5
18. Emeras, J.: The CEA Curie log. https://www.cse.huji.ac.il/labs/parallel/workload/l_cea_curie/index.html
19. Sandgren, A., Jack, M.: The HPC2N Seth log. https://www.cse.huji.ac.il/labs/parallel/workload/l_hpc2n/index.html
20. Feitelson, D.G.: Metrics for parallel job scheduling and their convergence. In: Feitelson, D.G., Rudolph, L. (eds.) JSSPP 2001. LNCS, vol. 2221, pp. 188–205. Springer, Heidelberg (2001). https://doi.org/10.1007/3-540-45540-X_11
21. Chiang, S.-H., Arpaci-Dusseau, A., Vernon, M.K.: The impact of more accurate requested runtimes on production job scheduling performance. In: Feitelson, D.G., Rudolph, L., Schwiegelshohn, U. (eds.) JSSPP 2002. LNCS, vol. 2537, pp. 103–127. Springer, Heidelberg (2002). https://doi.org/10.1007/3-540-36180-4_7

22. Fan, Y., et al.: Scheduling beyond CPUs for HPC. In: Proceedings of the 28th International Symposium on High-Performance Parallel and Distributed Computing, pp. 97–108. ACM (2019)
23. Freund, Y., Schapire, R.E.: A decision-theoretic generalization of on-line learning and an application to boosting. J. Comput. Syst. Sci. **55**(1), 119–139 (1997)
24. Bühlmann, P., Hothorn, T.: Boosting algorithms: regularization, prediction and model fitting. Stat. Sci. **22** (2008). https://doi.org/10.1214/07-STS242
25. Tsafrir, D.: Using inaccurate estimates accurately. In: Frachtenberg, E., Schwiegelshohn, U. (eds.) JSSPP 2010. LNCS, vol. 6253, pp. 208–221. Springer, Heidelberg (2010). https://doi.org/10.1007/978-3-642-16505-4_12
26. COARE workload in SWF. https://github.com/erangvee/slurm_sim_vanilla/blob/master/ASTI-COARE-2018-cln.swf
27. Yoo, A.B., Jette, M.A., Grondona, M.: SLURM: simple Linux utility for resource management. In: Feitelson, D., Rudolph, L., Schwiegelshohn, U. (eds.) JSSPP 2003. LNCS, vol. 2862, pp. 44–60. Springer, Heidelberg (2003). https://doi.org/10.1007/10968987_3
28. Simakov, N.A., et al.: A Slurm simulator: implementation and parametric analysis. In: Jarvis, S., Wright, S., Hammond, S. (eds.) PMBS 2017. LNCS, vol. 10724, pp. 197–217. Springer, Cham (2018). https://doi.org/10.1007/978-3-319-72971-8_10
29. Lewis, R.J.: An introduction to classification and regression tree (CART) analysis. In: Annual Meeting of the Society for Academic Emergency Medicine in San Francisco, California, vol. 14 (2000)
30. You, H., Zhang, H.: Comprehensive workload analysis and modeling of a petascale supercomputer. In: Cirne, W., Desai, N., Frachtenberg, E., Schwiegelshohn, U. (eds.) JSSPP 2012. LNCS, vol. 7698, pp. 253–271. Springer, Heidelberg (2013). https://doi.org/10.1007/978-3-642-35867-8_14

Author Index

Printed in the United States
By Bookmasters